DINO WARS

Copyright © 2005 Marshall Editions
Conceived, edited and designed by Marshall Editions
The Old Brewery, 6 Blundell Street, London N7 9BH, UK
www.quarto.com

Publisher: Richard Green
Commissioning editor: Claudia Martin
Art direction: Ivo Marloh
Editor: Sharon Hynes
Designer: Claire Harvey
Production: Nikki Ingram

Published in 2005 by Harry N. Abrams, Incorporated, New York.

ISBN 0-8109-9194-2

Library of Congress Cataloging-in-Publication Data available on request

Originated in Hong Kong by Modern Age
Printed and bound in China by Midas Printing International Limited

2 4 6 8 10 9 7 5 3 1

Harry N. Abrams, Inc.
100 Fifth Avenue
New York, NY 10011
www.abramsbooks.com

Abrams is a subsidiary of

DINO WARS

Jinny Johnson

Consultant: Professor Michael J. Benton

Harry N. Abrams, Inc., Publishers

6–13 .... 1 THE RULES OF ENGAGEMENT
8 ....The Basics
10 ....Competitor Group 1:
Early Reptiles
12 ....Competitor Group 2: Dinosaurs

14–23 .. 2 PALEOZOIC PUNCHES
16 ....Combat Zone: The Carboniferous
and Permian Periods
18 ....Petrolacosaurus & Edaphosaurus
20 ....Moschops vs. Lycaenops
22 ....Pareiasaurus & Hovasaurus

24–45 .. 3 TRIASSIC TUSSLES
26 ....Combat Zone:
The Triassic Period
28 ....Euparkeria & Placodus
30 ....Erythrosuchus vs. Cynognathus
32 ....Marasuchus & Shonisaurus
34 ....Coelophysis
36 ....Desmatosuchus & Eudimorphodon

38 ....Special Skill: Flight
40 ....Pistosaurus & Plateosaurus
42 ....Eoraptor vs. Herrerasaurus
44 ....Hypsognathus & Proganochelys

46–79 .. 4 JURASSIC JOUSTS
48 ....Combat Zone:
The Jurassic Period
50 ....Teleosaurus & Scutellosaurus
52 ....Special Skill: Swimming
54 ....Lesothosaurus & Cryolophosaurus
56 ....Kentrosaurus vs. Allosaurus
58 ....Lufengosaurus & Lexovisaurus
60 ....Stegosaurus
62 ....Mamenchisaurus & Pterodaustro
64 ....Battle Tactic: Speed
66 ....Ophthalmosaurus & Tuojiangosaurus
68 ....Diplodocus
70 ....Apatosaurus & Rhamphorhynchus
72 ....Brachiosaurus vs. Ceratosaurus
74 ....Seismosaurus & Scaphognathus

CONT

76 .... Battle Tactic: Strength
78 .... Megalosaurus

80–135 5 CRETACEOUS CLASHES

82 .... Combat Zone:
          The Cretaceous Period
84 .... Leaellynasaura & Kronosaurus
86 .... Iguanodon
88 .... Amargasaurus & Sauropelta
90 .... Deinonychus vs. Hypsilophodon
92 .... Ouranosaurus & Wuerhosaurus
94 .... Carnotaurus & Pentaceratops
96 .... Euoplocephalus & Dromaeosaurus
98 .... Battle Tactic: Armor
100 ...... Archelon & Deinosuchus
102 ...... Gallimimus vs. Tarbosaurus
104 ...... Protoceratops & Chasmosaurus
106 ...... Quetzalcoatlus & Giganotosaurus
108 ...... Battle Tactic: Scariness
110 ...... Velociraptor & Suchomimus
112 .... Dromiceiomimus & Parasaurolophus

114 .... Mosasaurus Hoffmani
116 .... Therizinosaurus & Daspletosaurus
118 ...... Battle Tactic: Agility
120 ...... Pachycephalosaurus & Torosaurus
122 ...... Panoplosaurus & Tsintaosaurus
124 ...... Special Skill: Herd Instinct
126 ...... Styracosaurus & Shantungosaurus
128 ...... Triceratops
130 ...... Tyrannosaurus
132 ...... Tyrannosaurus vs. Triceratops
134 ...... Dinosaurs vs. Extinction

136 ...... Score Table
138 ...... Glossary
140 ...... Index
144 ...... Illustration Credits

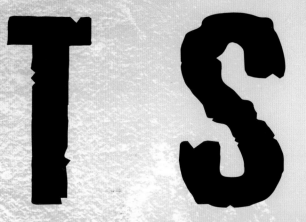

ENTS

THE RULES OF

ENGAGEMENT

THE BASICS

Millions of years before the first humans evolved, life on Earth was dominated by dinosaurs and other amazing reptiles. Then, as now, animals struggled to find enough food to eat and to protect themselves from danger. Some fed on plants; others preyed on creatures smaller than themselves. The largest and fiercest took part in terrifying battles in a desperate bid to stay alive. In this book we look at the strengths and weaknesses of many of these animals, and how they might have fared when pitted against one another in a battle to the death.

Dinosaurs disappeared from Earth at least 60 million years before the first humans lived, so nobody has ever seen a live dinosaur. But scientists can find out a great deal about dinosaurs by looking at the many fossilized remains that have been found. Their teeth show what sort of food a dinosaur ate: sharp, jagged-edged teeth belonged to meat-eaters, while plant-eaters had broad, blunt teeth. Marks on fossil bones show where muscles were attached and help experts work out the shape of the living animal. Recently fossils have been found revealing that some dinosaurs had a covering of feathers, just like birds today.

Scientists can also get an idea of how dinosaurs may have fed, moved, and cared for their young by comparing them with living animals. For example, today's big plant-eaters, such as zebras and antelopes, live in herds, which makes paleontologists believe that big plant-eating dinosaurs probably did, too. And it's likely that dinosaurs had similar coloration and patterns on their skin—as camouflage to help blend into the environment or to help attract a mate—to animals living similar lifestyles today. This also helps us work out how they may have looked.

COMBAT ZONES

⬆ PALEOZOIC

The Paleozoic era began 550 million years ago and included the Cambrian, Ordovician, Silurian, Devonian, and then finally the Carboniferous and Permian periods, when our first combatants, the early reptiles, appeared.

⬆ TRIASSIC

The Triassic period began about 250 million years ago and lasted until 200 million years ago. It was during this period that the first dinosaurs evolved.

⬅ JURASSIC

The Jurassic period began 200 million years ago and lasted until 146 million years ago.

⬇ CRETACEOUS

The Cretaceous began 146 million years ago and ended 65 million years ago. By then all the dinosaurs had disappeared from Earth.

BATTLE TACTICS

⬊ STRENGTH

For the biggest dinosaurs, strength was a major weapon, whether for attacking prey or for defending themselves from enemies.

🏃 ARMOR

Some dinosaurs and other reptiles had heavy body armor, made of plates of bone, as well as spikes and horns, which helped to protect them in battles with other animals.

⏱ SPEED

Being able to move fast was sometimes even more important than being strong or well armored—fast runners could escape from danger, or move quickly to capture prey.

⬃ AGILITY

Although many dinosaurs were lumbering creatures, others were amazingly agile, able to dart and leap as they attacked prey or defended themselves.

☠ SCARINESS

Sheer size made many dinosaurs a terrifying sight. Even many much smaller reptiles were scary because of their sharp teeth and their ferocious fighting skills.

★ SPECIAL SKILLS

Many dinosaurs and other reptiles had particularly useful abilities, such as flight or a fantastic sense of smell or sight.

DANGER LEVEL

DANGER LEVEL (7) Each animal is given an overall danger-level rating. This is the total of the scores for each battle tactic divided by six to give an average score. See p.136 for the highest scorers.

COMPETITOR GROUP 1: EARLY REPTILES

The first reptiles appeared 100 million years before dinosaurs, during the Late Carboniferous. They evolved from amphibians, creatures like frogs and salamanders that spent at least part of their lives in water. Reptiles were the first vertebrates (animals with backbones) to live on land. Unlike the mighty dinosaurs, which came later, the earliest reptiles were mostly small creatures, similar to lizards today. They fed on insects and spiders, which they snapped up in their small, sharp teeth.

The very first reptiles were called anapsids. They had heavy boxlike skulls with openings only for the eyes and nostrils. Later came diapsid and synapsid reptiles. These had lighter skulls with extra openings and much more powerful jaw muscles, which enabled them to bite more efficiently.

THE FIRST REPTILES

Speedy little Hylonomus was one of the first reptiles and one of the earliest of all land animals. It measured only about 8 in (20 cm) in total and had a long lizardlike body and a slender tail. Hylonomus lived in North America more than 300 million years ago.

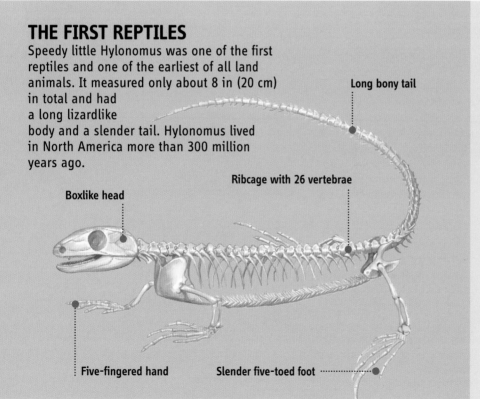

Long bony tail

Ribcage with 26 vertebrae

Boxlike head

Five-fingered hand

Slender five-toed foot

A SHELLED EGG

An amphibian egg has to be laid in water. It has no shell, only a jelly-like coating which has to be kept moist. Reptile eggs can be laid on land. They have a tough shell, which protects the growing baby inside and keeps the egg from drying out.

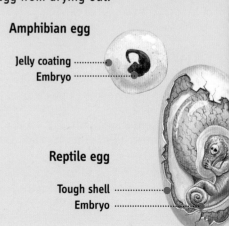

Amphibian egg

Jelly coating

Embryo

Reptile egg

Tough shell

Embryo

KEY TYPES OF EARLY REPTILES

Early reptiles: Hylonomus
The first reptiles, such as Hylonomus, belonged to a group called anapsids and had a boxlike skull. They evolved during the Late Carboniferous.

Mammal-like reptiles: Dicynodon
The first mammal-like reptiles (see p.21) lived some 300 million years ago. They were the biggest, fiercest land animals on Earth before the appearance of the dinosaurs. But they were all extinct by the middle of the Jurassic.

Ichthyosaur: Stenopterygius
Ichthyosaurs were marine reptiles and were perfectly adapted to life in the sea. They were shaped very like dolphins today and could swim fast as they hunted fish and squid.

Crocodiles: Teleosaurus
Crocodiles lived at the same time as dinosaurs and they have hardly changed to this day. They have well-armored bodies, short legs, and a long tail, and are very fierce hunters.

Lizards: Ardeosaurus
The first lizards lived in the mid-Jurassic, about 175 million years ago. There are still lots of different kinds of lizards, which look very similar to Ardeosaurus, in the world today.

Turtles: Archelon
Turtles, which are anapsids, like the very earliest reptiles, first appeared in the Late Triassic, 220 million years ago. Triassic turtles had a hard shell, just like turtles and tortoises today.

Flying reptiles: Pteranodon
Pterosaurs evolved in the Late Triassic, 220 million years ago, and were the first creatures to take to life in the air. They flew on wings made of skin, which were attached to their long finger bones and their legs.

COMPETITOR GROUP 2: DINOSAURS

Dinosaurs were the most amazing reptiles that have ever lived. The first dinosaurs lived during the Late Triassic. They ruled the world for more than 150 million years, but they all died out at the end of the Cretaceous period, about 65 million years ago.

The biggest dinosaurs were more than 100 feet (30 meters) long, some of the most gigantic creatures that ever walked the Earth. But not all were ferocious flesh-eating monsters. Many of the largest dinosaurs ate only plants. Others were light, speedy creatures only about the size of a chicken. We know there were at least 500 different kinds of dinosaurs, but there may have been many more that no one knows about yet.

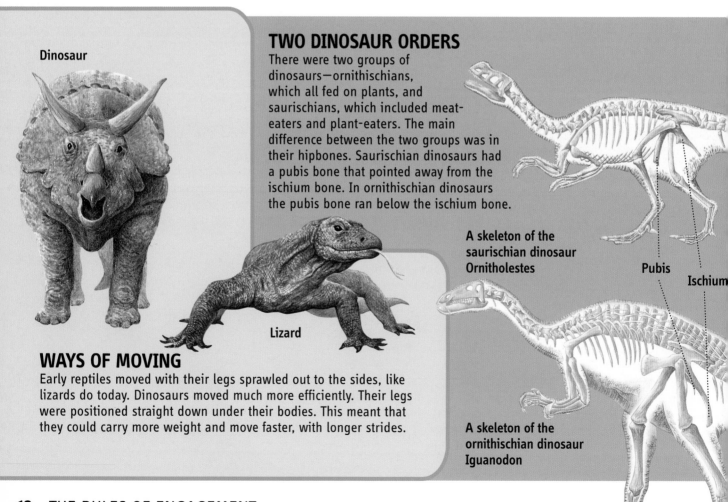

Dinosaur

TWO DINOSAUR ORDERS

There were two groups of dinosaurs—ornithischians, which all fed on plants, and saurischians, which included meat-eaters and plant-eaters. The main difference between the two groups was in their hipbones. Saurischian dinosaurs had a pubis bone that pointed away from the ischium bone. In ornithischian dinosaurs the pubis bone ran below the ischium bone.

A skeleton of the saurischian dinosaur Ornitholestes

Pubis

Ischium

Lizard

WAYS OF MOVING

Early reptiles moved with their legs sprawled out to the sides, like lizards do today. Dinosaurs moved much more efficiently. Their legs were positioned straight down under their bodies. This meant that they could carry more weight and move faster, with longer strides.

A skeleton of the ornithischian dinosaur Iguanodon

KEY TYPES OF DINOSAURS

Saurischians

Carnosaurs
This group included some of the best known of all dinosaurs—the tyrannosaurs and hunters such as Allosaurus. They were all large creatures with big heads and jaws lined with deadly, razor-sharp teeth.

Ornithomimids
These dinosaurs looked very like the ostriches of today. They could run fast on their long back legs.

Dromaeosaurs
Dromaeosaurs were fast runners too, but were much fiercer than ornithomimids. They had a lethal claw on each foot, which they could use as weapons.

Coelurosaurs
These were fast-moving hunters with slender legs and strong claws on their hands and feet.

Sauropods
These huge, long-necked plant-eaters were the giants of the dinosaur world. They included mighty creatures such as Brachiosaurus, Diplodocus, and Seismosaurus. The biggest were well over 50 feet (15 meters) long.

Ornithischians

Armored dinosaurs
The dinosaurs in this group—ankylosaurs and nodosaurs—were all heavily armored. Most had back, sides, and tail covered with flat plates of bone set into the thick skin.

Stegosaurs
Stegosaurs had double rows of bony plates set all down the back and sharp spikes lining the tail.

Boneheaded dinosaurs
A dome-shaped skull was the most unusual feature of the dinosaurs in this group. Some also had bones and spikes on the head.

Horned dinosaurs
These dinosaurs had heavily armored bodies with huge curving horns on the head and a sheet of bone curving out from the back of the skull.

Duckbilled dinosaurs
Duckbills were among the most common dinosaurs. All had a beaklike snout and most had horns or crests on their heads.

Iguanodons
These large plant-eating dinosaurs had a sharp thumb spike on each hand that could be bent across the palm for holding food.

PALEOZOIC

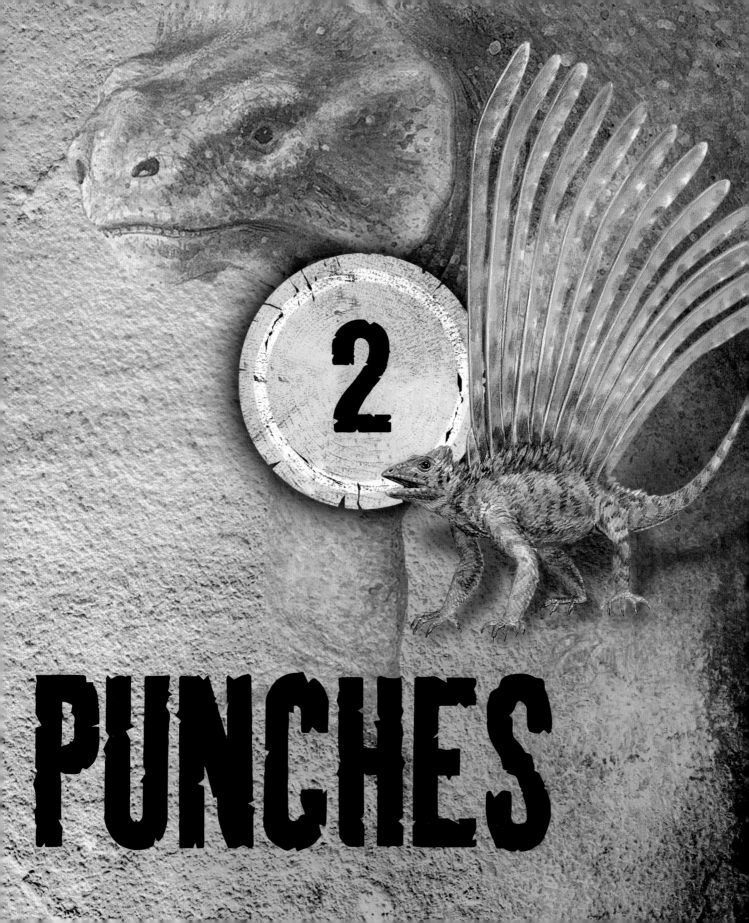

2

PUNCHES

COMBAT ZONE: THE CARBONIFEROUS AND PERMIAN PERIODS

The first reptiles lived in the Carboniferous period, which began about 360 million years ago. At the beginning of the Carboniferous, the world's climate was mostly warm and wet, but it gradually became cooler and more seasonal. Thick forests of horsetails, tree ferns, and club mosses grew. The first insects, such as giant dragonflies, darted among the plants—and were gobbled up by early reptiles such as Hylonomus. The word Carboniferous means "coal-bearing." At this time the world's first coal deposits were formed from the huge amounts of plant debris that had collected in the forests over millions of years.

The Permian period, which followed the Carboniferous, began about 290 million years ago. There were more and more reptiles at this time, but still no dinosaurs. The world's landmasses moved even closer together than they'd been in the Carboniferous to make one supercontinent—Pangaea. In the northern half of the world, the climate was very hot and dry and many of the lush Carboniferous forests disappeared. The southern half of the world was much colder. Conifers were the most common plants. By the end of the Permian large mammal-like reptiles (see p.21) were the dominant land animals.

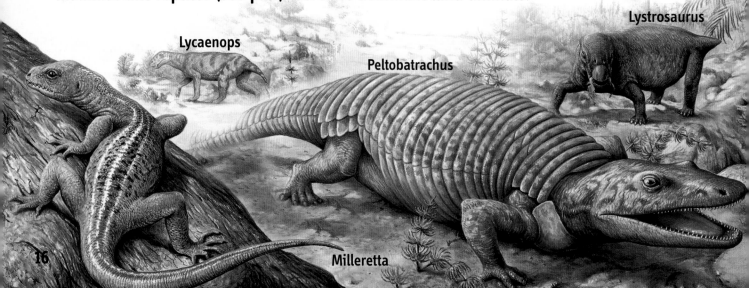

Lystrosaurus

Lycaenops

Peltobatrachus

Milleretta

THE CARBONIFEROUS WORLD

At this time the world was divided into two huge landmasses—Laurentia in the north and Gondwana in the south. During the Carboniferous, Gondwana moved clockwise. The land now known as India, Australia, and Antarctica moved south, and what is now South America and Africa moved north.

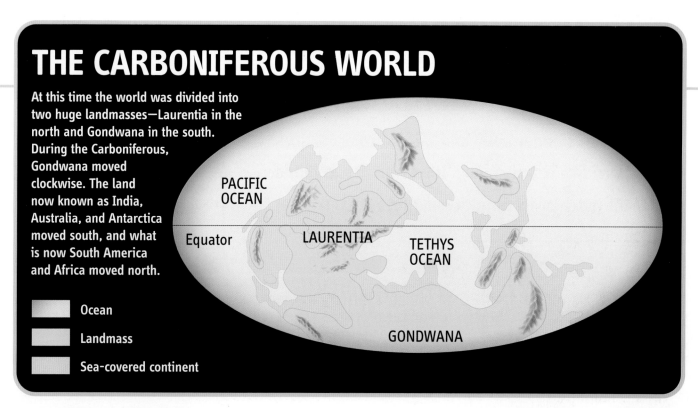

PACIFIC OCEAN

Equator

LAURENTIA

TETHYS OCEAN

GONDWANA

Ocean

Landmass

Sea-covered continent

THE PERMIAN LANDSCAPE

This Permian landscape, in the area that is now South Africa, is very dry, with scattered plants such as horsetails, ginkgos, and the first cycads. Fierce Lycaenops has arrived on the scene, threatening plant-eating reptiles such as Robertia and Dicynodon as they feed by the water's edge.

Dicynodon

Lycaenops

Robertia

Procynosuchus

PETROLACOSAURUS
aka SNAPPER

DANGER LEVEL 3.5

With its long, slender body and tail, Petrolacosaurus looked very like lizards today. It was an active hunter and spent much of its time chasing insects and other small creatures.

BONUS FEATURE:
SHARP TEETH
Its sharp, pointed teeth allowed this little reptile to gobble up plenty of insects.

VITAL STATISTICS
Order: Araeoscelidia
Family: Petrolacosauridae
Period: Late Carboniferous
Home territory: North America: Kansas
Habitat: Dry plains
Size: 16 in (40 cm) long

DISTINGUISHING FEATURES
Petrolacosaurus was one of the earliest diapsid reptiles—reptiles with two openings on each side of the skull that made its head lighter and its jaws stronger.

COMBAT HISTORY
Petrolacosaurus would win every time against insects, but could easily be snapped up by larger reptiles looking for a meal. Fortunately, it could often scuttle speedily away from its enemies.

STRENGTH: 1
Too small to be strong, Petrolacosaurus would have had to make up for its lack of muscle with lightning-fast reflexes.

ARMOR: 1
Petrolacosaurus had no body armor and relied on speed for protection.

SPEED: 7
This little reptile needed to be a fast runner to chase and catch insects as they darted from plant to plant.

AGILITY: 7
Petrolacosaurus was agile too, able to scurry up tree trunks and over rocks in pursuit of prey.

SCARINESS: 1
This reptile was too small to be scary—unless you were an insect!

SPECIAL SKILLS: 4
As well as regular sharp teeth, Petrolacosaurus made use of a pair of larger canine teeth in its top jaw, ideal for impaling and killing its prey.

EDAPHOSAURUS
aka SHOW-OFF

DANGER LEVEL
3.8

With the huge bloodred sail-like crest on its back, Edaphosaurus was a spectacular sight. This big, bulky animal fed on plants, which it chopped with powerful jaws lined with closely packed teeth.

BONUS FEATURE:
THE SAIL
This reptile's strange sail was in fact a very useful device that helped it keep its temperature constant whatever the weather!

VITAL STATISTICS
Order: Pelycosauria
Family: Edaphosauridae
Period: Early Permian
Home territory: Europe, North America: Texas
Habitat: Wet areas near swamps and lakes
Size: 10 ft (3 m) long

DISTINGUISHING FEATURES
The sail on Edaphosaurus's back was made up of enormously long spines that extended from the backbone and were covered with skin.

COMBAT HISTORY
This bulky, slow-moving creature was not built for fighting and preferred to stay out of trouble. Fortunately, its impressive sail would have made it a daunting prospect for most predators.

STRENGTH: 5
Edaphosaurus had a big, strong body and head, but there was little power in its short arms and legs.

ARMOR: 5
Edaphosaurus had no armor on its body, but its spiny sail would have given some protection from enemies.

SPEED: 1
This reptile was not built for speed, and depended on its bulk for defense.

AGILITY: 1
Edaphosaurus was a heavy animal, weighing up to about 660 lb (300 kg), and not at all agile in its movements.

SCARINESS: 5
Its size, combined with its colorful sail, would have been enough to put off many predators.

SPECIAL SKILLS: 6
Edaphosaurus's sail may have helped it control its body temperature. When it was cold, Edaphosaurus could turn its sail toward the sun to warm the blood as it flowed through the skin on the sail. To cool down, it turned the sail away from the sun and into the wind.

THE
BATTLE

TIME:
Late Permian

PLACE:
South Africa

WINNER:
Lycaenops

MOSCHOPS
VS. LYCAENOPS

Size doesn't always matter. As a massive Moschops quietly feeds on its favorite plants, a pack of smaller reptiles, speedy, sharp-toothed Lycaenops, circles around it. Together they pounce. As one hunter leaps on its back and others go for its throat and belly, the gentle giant is soon overpowered by their vicious bites.

MOSCHOPS

Order: Dinocephalia
Family: Tapinocephalidae
Size: 15 ft (4.5 m) long

This plant-eater was a large, powerfully built animal. Its head was huge with extra-thick bones in the forehead, which would have protected it in head-butting battles.

MAMMAL-LIKE REPTILES

The first mammal-like reptiles lived during the Late Carboniferous, around 300 million years ago. Like mammals, they had three sets of teeth—incisors, canines, and molars—and an enlarged brain. The earliest species were small and lizardlike, but they soon evolved into larger, heavier creatures with strong jaws and sharp teeth. Some were fierce hunters, but others were plant-eaters. Mammal-like reptiles dominated life on Earth before the dinosaurs, but became extinct during the Jurassic period. The most advanced in the group were the therapsids, including Moschops, which were close to the direct ancestors of mammals today.

LYCAENOPS

Order: Gorgonopsia
Family: Gorgonopsidae
Size: 3 ft (90 cm) long

Although small, this reptile could move swiftly and was a fierce hunter. It probably worked in a pack, using its strong jaws and large, daggerlike teeth to tear prey apart.

PAREIASAURUS

aka BONY

DANGER LEVEL **4.8**

One of the largest of all the early reptiles, Pareiasaurus was a heavy-bodied animal with massive trunklike legs to support its bulk. Despite its fearsome appearance, this reptile was a plant-eater and preferred to stay out of trouble.

VITAL STATISTICS
Order: Pareiasauria
Family: Pareiasauridae
Period: Middle Permian
Home territory: Africa, Russia
Habitat: Dry scrubland
Size: 8 ft (2.5 m) long

DISTINGUISHING FEATURES
Pareiasaurus had a large head studded with spikes and warty lumps. Its jaws were lined with plenty of small teeth with serrated edges for cutting and chewing tough plant food.

COMBAT HISTORY
As one of the largest animals of its day, Pareiasaurus had few enemies and would have been able to win most contests by brute force.

STRENGTH: 7
Burly Pareiasaurus was very strong, able to stand its ground against most attackers.

ARMOR: 8
Heavy plates of bone set into the skin on its back gave this reptile excellent protection from sharp-toothed hunters.

SPEED: 1
Speed was not an option for Pareiasaurus. Its body was too heavy and its legs were built for support, not fast movement.

AGILITY: 1
This big reptile was certainly not agile and could not leap or stand up on its back legs.

SCARINESS: 8
With its large spiked head, Pareiasaurus would have been an awesome sight, and not something most other Permian reptiles would want to tackle.

SPECIAL SKILLS: 4
Like most bullies, Pareiasaurus didn't have many genuine skills, but it definitely knew how to use its size to intimidate.

HOVASAURUS
aka GULPER

Hovasaurus was a swimming reptile with a slender lizardlike body and a very long tail. It lived in lakes and rivers, where it preyed on fish and other water creatures. This reptile also had a strange but highly useful special skill.

VITAL STATISTICS
Order: Lepidosauromorpha
Family: Tangasauridae
Period: Late Permian
Home territory: Africa: Madagascar
Habitat: Lakes and rivers
Size: 20 in (50 cm) long

DISTINGUISHING FEATURES
The tail of this reptile was about twice the length of its body and flattened from side to side. It made an ideal paddle for fast movement in water.

COMBAT HISTORY
Hovasaurus was an expert predator and could catch small fish with ease—but was no match for larger aquatic reptiles.

STRENGTH: 2
Hovasaurus was a strong swimmer but was too small and weedy to fight off any larger predators.

ARMOR: 0
This reptile had no body armor so had to escape quickly if attacked.

SPEED: 5
Hovasaurus's paddle-like tail helped it zip through the water at high speed.

AGILITY: 5
An agile swimmer, Hovasaurus could dive deep beneath the water surface as it pursued its prey.

SCARINESS: 1
This reptile was too small to scare anything but its prey— little fish and other tiny water-living creatures.

SPECIAL SKILLS: 5
Like some crocodiles today, Hovasaurus swallowed stones to help it sink quickly in the water when diving for prey or to help it stay under when feeding.

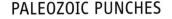

TRIASSIC

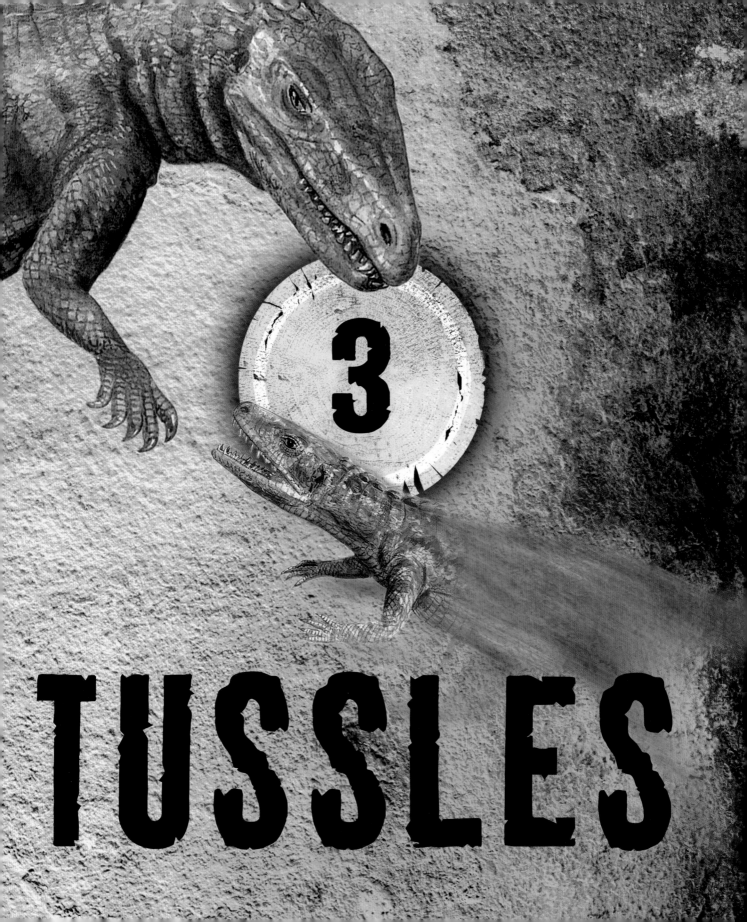

3

TUSSLES

COMBAT ZONE: THE TRIASSIC PERIOD

The Triassic period began about 250 million years ago. The supercontinent, Pangaea, lay across the equator. There were no ice caps and the climate was very warm, with little change from season to season. Large areas of land were a long distance from the sea and so were drier than they are now, causing vast deserts. Flowering plants or grasses had not yet evolved, so the landscape looked very different from the world today, and there were vast forests of conifers, ginkgos, and cycads. Huge ferns and horsetails also grew by lakes and rivers, and these were important foods for plant-eating reptiles, including the first dinosaurs.

Eudimorphodon, a flying reptile (pterosaur)

Plateosaurus, a prosauropod

Peteinosaurus, a flying reptile (pterosaur)

Liliensternus, a ceratosaur

Dragonfly

Terrestrisuchus, a crocodile

Shrewlike mammal

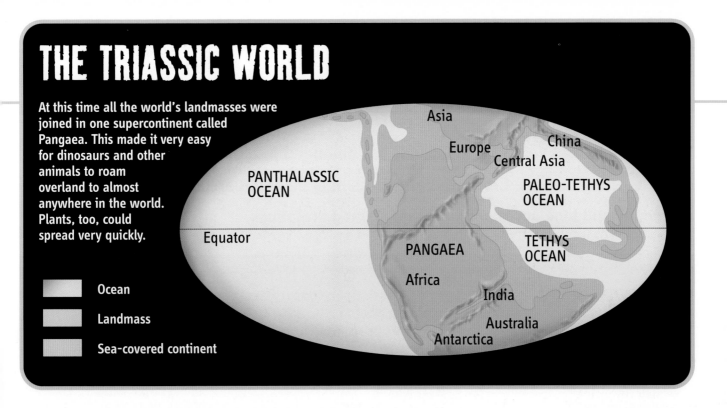

THE TRIASSIC WORLD

At this time all the world's landmasses were joined in one supercontinent called Pangaea. This made it very easy for dinosaurs and other animals to roam overland to almost anywhere in the world. Plants, too, could spread very quickly.

Asia

Europe

China

Central Asia

PANTHALASSIC OCEAN

PALEO-TETHYS OCEAN

Equator

TETHYS OCEAN

PANGAEA

Africa

India

Australia

Antarctica

Ocean

Landmass

Sea-covered continent

Insects such as beetles, grasshoppers, dragonflies, and cockroaches were plentiful, and the first flies and wasps appeared during the Triassic. During much of the Triassic, mammal-like reptiles and other early reptiles such as crocodiles dominated life on Earth. There were turtles and fish in rivers and lakes, and huge marine reptiles such as ichthyosaurs and nothosaurs lurked in the seas. But toward the end of the period, the first dinosaurs appeared and soon became the dominant large animals. They included some of the biggest land animals ever known to have lived on Earth.

THE TRIASSIC LANDSCAPE

In this Triassic woodland in what is now Europe, a group of mighty plant-eating dinosaurs munches on conifer branches. But their peace is disturbed by a hungry ceratosaur, Liliensternus, in search of food. Smaller creatures scurry in the undergrowth while huge pterosaurs soar overhead.

EUPARKERIA

aka NIPPER

DANGER LEVEL 4.2

Euparkeria looked very like a dinosaur but belonged to a group called archosaurs, or early ruling reptiles. Crocodiles and birds may be living archosaurian reptiles—crocodiles still look amazingly like their Triassic relatives.

VITAL STATISTICS

Order: Archosauria
Family: Euparkeriidae
Period: Early Triassic
Home territory: South Africa
Habitat: Dry plains
Size: 20 in (50 cm)

DISTINGUISHING FEATURES

Like many of the dinosaurs that came later, Euparkeria's front legs were much shorter than its back legs. Its long jaws were studded with many long sharp teeth.

COMBAT HISTORY

Euparkeria preyed on smaller reptiles and other creatures such as insects but would have been no match for larger dinosaurs. Its only hope was to run to escape its enemies.

STRENGTH: 2

Euparkeria was small but its jaws were remarkably powerful for its size.

ARMOR: 3

Euparkeria was lightly armored with a row of bony plates, which ran down its back and tail.

SPEED: 7

A fast runner, this little reptile could also race along on two legs.

AGILITY: 7

Euparkeria had a long tail, about half its body length, which helped balance its body when it ran on two legs.

SCARINESS: 3

For an insect or other small creature, Euparkeria—with toothy jaws gaping—would have been a scary sight.

SPECIAL SKILLS: 3

Strong jaws and sharp teeth with serrated edges made this small dinosaur a successful predator. But it knew its limits and stuck to picking on creatures way smaller than itself!

PLACODUS

aka CRUSHER

Placodus, like other placodonts, was happiest on seashores and swimming in shallow water rather than risking the open ocean. It fed on shellfish, which it prised from rocks with its specialized teeth.

VITAL STATISTICS

Order: Placodontia
Family: Placodontidae
Period: Early to Middle Triassic
Home territory: Europe
Habitat: Coasts and shallow seas
Size: 7 ft (2 m) long

DISTINGUISHING FEATURES

Placodus had a stocky body, short legs, and long flattened tail that may have acted like a paddle for swimming power.

COMBAT HISTORY

There was no need for Placodus to be aggressive or a good fighter to gather its shellfish prey. Although it did have some body armor, it would not have been able to put up much of a fight against a larger attacker.

STRENGTH: 5

Massive muscles gave this reptile very powerful jaws and great bite power for attacking hard-shelled prey.

ARMOR: 4

A row of bony knobs along its back, and belly ribs on its underside would have made Placodus harder to crunch!

SPEED: 3

Placodus was not ideally shaped for aquatic life, but it did have webbed feet and a strong tail to help it swim.

AGILITY: 1

This reptile's body was too bulky for it to be agile either on land or in water.

SCARINESS: 1

Although it was a big animal, Placodus would not have frightened anything, except the unlucky shellfish it prised from rocks.

SPECIAL SKILLS: 6

Placodus had an array of specialized teeth to help it gather its shellfish prey. At the front of its jaws were blunt teeth that stuck out and were used to pluck shellfish from rocks. Placodus then crushed its hard-shelled food with the broad back teeth.

THE BATTLE

TIME:
Early Triassic

PLACE:
South Africa

WINNER:
Erythrosuchus

ERYTHROSUCHUS VS. CYNOGNATHUS

Cynognathus hunts in packs, but one of these sharp-toothed predators has become separated from the rest of its group. A bigger stronger hunter, Erythrosuchus, is hot on Cynognathus's tail and seizes the smaller animal. Once Erythrosuchus has got its prey between its powerful jaws, the game is up—poor Cynognathus is speedily wolfed down.

ERYTHROSUCHUS

Order: Archosauria
Family: Erythrosuchidae
Size: 15 ft (4.5 m) long

Erythrosuchus was one of the biggest and fiercest hunters on land at this time. With its large head and powerful body, it would have been a formidable enemy.

EARLY RULING REPTILES

Ruling reptiles (or archosaurs) like Erythrosuchus were the dominant animals on Earth in the Early Triassic. There were a number of different groups. Among the earliest were the proterosuchids, which included crocodile-like hunters such as Proterosuchus. Later came creatures such as Ornithosuchus, which looked very like a dinosaur, and the water-living phytosaurs. These heavily armored creatures were the main predators in Triassic rivers. They had long jaws, ideal for catching fish. Aetosaurs, such as Desmatosuchus, were the first plant-eating archosaurs. Later archosaurs included the pterosaurs and the dinosaurs themselves.

CYNOGNATHUS

Suborder: Cynodontia
Family: Cynognathidae
Size: 3 ft (90 cm) long

Cynognathus had a powerful body. Its strong jaws were lined with three types of teeth—for cutting meat, stabbing prey, and chewing. This allowed it to deal with a varied diet.

MARASUCHUS

aka MOVER

DANGER LEVEL **4.5**

Light and speedy, Marasuchus was probably an ancestor of the dinosaurs. This sharp-toothed hunter preyed on smaller reptiles as well as insects, worms, and other small creatures.

VITAL STATISTICS
Order: Ornithodira
Family: Lagosuchidae
Period: Middle Triassic
Home territory: South America: Argentina
Habitat: All areas
Size: 4 ft (1 m) long

DISTINGUISHING FEATURES
Marasuchus's front legs were less than half the length of its back legs—a feature this reptile shared with many of the dinosaurs.

COMBAT HISTORY
Marasuchus would have only attacked smaller creatures and was not strong enough to defend itself against more powerful enemies. However, with its speed and agility, this reptile would have been able to escape from many dangerous situations.

STRENGTH: 3
Marasuchus was light but muscular with strong back legs and tail.

ARMOR: 0
Marasuchus had no body armor and would have depended on its speed for protection from enemies.

SPEED: 7
Long, slender legs show that this reptile was a fast runner, able to chase and catch insects as well as smaller reptiles.

AGILITY: 7
This lightly built animal was probably able to speed along on its two back legs as well as on all fours, balancing itself with its long tail.

SCARINESS: 4
Marasuchus was an effective hunter and surprisingly fierce for its size.

SPECIAL SKILLS: 6
Being able to move on two legs allowed Marasuchus to use its hands, equipped with sharp claws, to grab prey and cram tasty food into its mouth.

SHONISAURUS
aka SWIMMER

This oceangoing giant was the largest of all the ichthyosaurs. With its sleek streamlined body, it cut through the water at high speed attacking just about anything not quick enough to get out of its way.

VITAL STATISTICS
Order: Ichthyosauria
Family: Shonisauridae
Period: Late Triassic
Home territory: North America
Habitat: The seas
Size: 45 ft (14 m) long

DISTINGUISHING FEATURES
Shonisaurus had extremely long jaws, with teeth only at the front. The teeth were very sharp, allowing the ichthyosaur to seize hold of slippery prey.

COMBAT HISTORY
This huge ichthyosaur was a top predator in the sea. It probably traveled in packs, hunting prey such as fish and squid, which it snatched from the water and swallowed whole.

STRENGTH: 8
A strong, powerful reptile, Shonisaurus had no equal in Triassic seas.

ARMOR: 2
Shonisaurus had no body armor, but its layers of blubber would have given it some protection from anything silly enough to attack.

SPEED: 8
Propelling itself with its powerful tail, Shonisaurus could swim at speeds of up to 25 miles (40 km) per hour.

AGILITY: 8
Despite its size, Shonisaurus was very agile in the water, able to turn itself and steer with its paddle-like fins.

SCARINESS: 8
Sheer bulk made this ichthyosaur a very scary sight. No other creature would want to get in its way.

SPECIAL SKILLS: 6
Shonisaurus was perfectly designed for life as a sea-living predator. An expert swimmer armed with sharp teeth, it could catch any prey it wanted.

COELOPHYSIS
aka SPEEDY

One of the earliest dinosaurs, Coelophysis was a fast-moving, merciless hunter. It seized fish from Triassic rivers, worked in packs to attack much larger creatures, and may even have gobbled up the young of its own kind.

VITAL STATISTICS
Order: Saurischia
Family: Coelophysidae
Period: Late Triassic
Home territory: North America: Connecticut, New Mexico
Habitat: Forests, close to streams and lakes
Size: Up to 15 ft (4.5 m) long

DISTINGUISHING FEATURES
One of the reasons Coelophysis was very quick and agile was that its leg bones were so light they were almost hollow. This reduced the dinosaur's body weight and made it easier for it to move fast.

COMBAT HISTORY
Coelophysis was a skilled hunter, clever enough to catch many different kinds of prey. In packs, these small dinosaurs could probably overcome animals much larger than themselves.

STRENGTH: 1
This dinosaur would have had to rely on its agility rather than strength to win its battles.

ARMOR: 0
Coelophysis had no body armor, but could easily outrun most larger hunters.

SPEED: 7
Coeolphysis could probably race along at 30 miles (50 km) an hour, overtaking many other animals of the time.

AGILITY: 8
Light and long-legged Coelophysis was very nimble on its feet. It used its lengthy tail for balance, constantly adjusting it to keep itself steady.

SCARINESS: 7
Coelophysis wasn't large, but a pack of these hunters with their grasping hands and sharp teeth must have been a fearsome sight.

SPECIAL SKILLS: 7
This hunter's narrow jaws were packed with razor-sharp teeth. At the front of the jaws were small, sharp teeth for seizing prey such as fish. Further back were larger teeth with serrated edges—ideal for slicing through even the gristliest of flesh!

Animals scatter as a pack of Coelophysis arrives at a drying lake. Mighty toothed jaws agape, the Coelophysis move on their back legs, leaving their sharp-clawed hands free for grasping prey.

DESMATOSUCHUS
aka SHOULDERS

This heavily armored reptile may have looked fierce but in fact was a harmless plant-eater. A gentle giant, it was one of the largest animals of the Late Triassic.

BONUS FEATURE:
DEADLY SPIKES
Large sharp spikes projecting from its shoulders made Desmatosuchus hard to attack.

VITAL STATISTICS
Order: Crurotarsi
Family: Stagonolepididae
Period: Late Triassic
Home territory: North America: Texas
Habitat: All areas
Size: 15 ft (4.5 m) long

DISTINGUISHING FEATURES
This reptile's head was surprisingly small for its huge armor-plated body.

COMBAT HISTORY
Few creatures would have dared attack this tanklike, spiky reptile, but if under threat Desmatosuchus would have relied on its armor to protect it from sharp teeth and claws.

STRENGTH: 4
Big and powerful, this reptile had a strong, muscular body—but its jaws and teeth were surprisingly weak.

ARMOR: 7
Massive plates of bone protected Desmatosuchus's body, and a pair of spikes, up to 17 inches (45 cm) long, stuck out from its shoulders. These were certainly enough to put off most predators!

SPEED: 1
With its short legs and heavy body, Desmatosuchus could not move fast and depended on its body armor for protection.

AGILITY: 1
Its heavy body armor made it hard for this reptile to change direction or maneuver its body.

SCARINESS: 6
With its sharp shoulder spikes, Desmatosuchus looked a lot fiercer than it really was. Fortunately many animals wouldn't venture close enough to find out.

SPECIAL SKILLS: 6
Although slow-moving and docile, Desmatosuchus knew how to use its impressive bulk and body armor to maximum effect—by literally turning its back on its enemies!

EUDIMORPHODON
aka PILOT

One of the earliest pterosaurs, Eudimorphodon was an expert hunter. This flying reptile soared over the sea, its large eyes always alert for any sign of its fish prey.

BONUS FEATURE:
THE RUDDER
The diamond-shaped flap at the tip of its tail may have helped this pterosaur change direction in the air.

VITAL STATISTICS
Order: Pterosauria
Family: Dimorphodontidae
Period: Late Triassic
Home territory: Europe: Italy
Habitat: Open sea and coastal cliffs
Size: 29 in (75 cm) from wingtip to wingtip, 25 in (60 cm) long, nose to tail

DISTINGUISHING FEATURES
Eudimorphodon had a long bony tail that made up about half its total length. Its jaws were short, compared with those of later pterosaurs, and lined with two sorts of teeth—long peglike teeth at the front, and short, broader teeth at the back.

COMBAT HISTORY
Pterosaurs were the rulers of the skies in Triassic times and their only enemies were larger pterosaurs. On land, however, pterosaurs moved quite awkwardly and would have been much more vulnerable to attack by other reptiles.

STRENGTH: 4
Eudimorphodon had powerful wing muscles and strong jaws, but its body was small and light.

ARMOR: 0
Pterosaurs had no body armor and depended on their ability to fly swiftly away for protection.

SPEED: 7
In the air Eudimorphodon was a speedy, powerful flier. On land it moved more slowly, crawling on all fours with the help of the claws on its wings as well as its feet.

AGILITY: 6
Like all pterosaurs, Eudimorphodon was very agile in the air, able to swoop and dive and maneuver its body with ease.

SCARINESS: 6
With their big wings and gaping jaws, pterosaurs were awe-inspiring hunters.

★ SPECIAL SKILLS: 7
Eudimorphodon probably flew low over the sea, keeping its highly effective eyes trained on the surface for any sign of prey. It would have held its long tail out behind it to balance its body in flight.

SPECIAL SKILL: FLIGHT

The first flying reptiles, pterosaurs, lived in the Late Triassic at the same time as the earliest dinosaurs. They were the first vertebrates (animals with backbones) to take to life in the air.

Several different kinds of pterosaurs glide on outstretched wings over the ocean searching for fish. Other pterosaurs perch on the rocks using the claws on their wings as well as their feet to move around on all fours.

There were at least 120 different kinds of pterosaurs but they were all extinct by the end of the Cretaceous. All had wings that were attached to the sides of the pterosaur's body and to the extra-long fourth finger on each hand. There were two main groups of pterosaurs. First came rhamphorhynchoids, which had a short neck and long tail. The later pterodactyloids were much larger and most had a short tail and long neck.

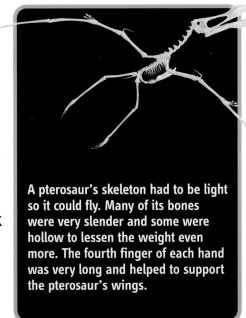

A pterosaur's skeleton had to be light so it could fly. Many of its bones were very slender and some were hollow to lessen the weight even more. The fourth finger of each hand was very long and helped to support the pterosaur's wings.

Anhanguera was very skilled at catching fish. This pterosaur soared over the sea until it spotted a fish, swooped down to seize it from the water, then flew off to devour its meal.

PISTOSAURUS
aka PADDLES

Pistosaurus was a nothosaur—a long-necked, fish-eating reptile. With its paddle-like limbs and webbed feet it was an expert swimmer, ideally suited to life in the sea.

VITAL STATISTICS
Order: Plesiosauria
Family: Pistosauridae
Period: Triassic
Home territory: Europe
Habitat: The seas
Size: 9 ft (2.7 m) long

DISTINGUISHING FEATURES
Like seals today, nothosaurs spent much of their time in water, but they were still air-breathing animals. They came to the surface to breathe and may have sometimes rested on rocks.

COMBAT HISTORY
Few fish could escape this nothosaur's deadly jaws, but it would struggle in a battle with a larger marine reptile such as mighty Shonisaurus.

STRENGTH: 1
Pistosaurus was not particularly strong and its long slender neck would have been disastrously easy to attack and damage.

ARMOR: 0
Pistosaurus had no body armor to protect it from larger predators.

SPEED: 5
Like other nothosaurs, Pistosaurus propelled itself through the water with its limbs and tail.

AGILITY: 6
This nothosaur's long body, neck, and tail were all very flexible so it could twist and turn with ease as it chased its prey.

SCARINESS: 3
To a fish, Pistosaurus was a deadly enemy, but it would not have been able to attack larger animals.

SPECIAL SKILLS: 7
Pistosaurus's long, slender jaws were lined with sharp interlocking teeth, making a perfect fish trap.

PLATEOSAURUS
aka THE TAIL

A massive tail made up about half the length of this huge dinosaur. But good-natured Plateosaurus was a plant-eater and got no more daring than rearing up on two legs to munch the leaves of tall trees.

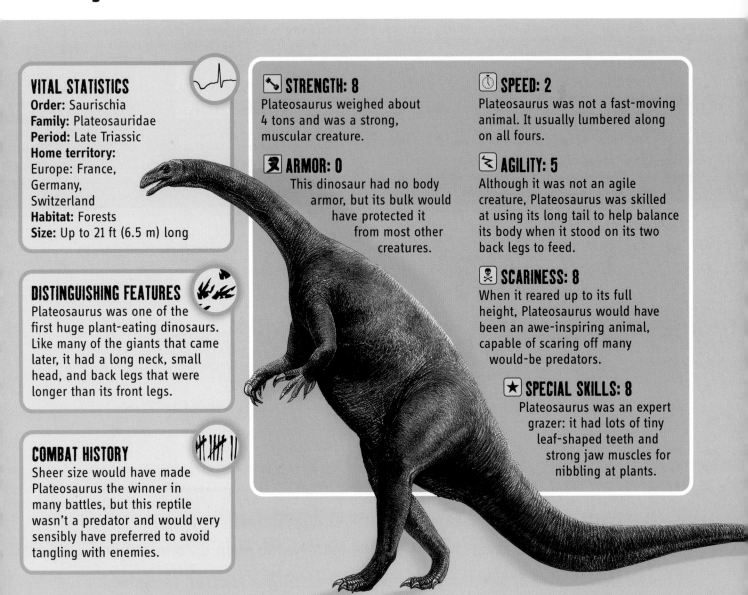

VITAL STATISTICS
Order: Saurischia
Family: Plateosauridae
Period: Late Triassic
Home territory:
Europe: France,
Germany,
Switzerland
Habitat: Forests
Size: Up to 21 ft (6.5 m) long

DISTINGUISHING FEATURES
Plateosaurus was one of the first huge plant-eating dinosaurs. Like many of the giants that came later, it had a long neck, small head, and back legs that were longer than its front legs.

COMBAT HISTORY
Sheer size would have made Plateosaurus the winner in many battles, but this reptile wasn't a predator and would very sensibly have preferred to avoid tangling with enemies.

STRENGTH: 8
Plateosaurus weighed about 4 tons and was a strong, muscular creature.

ARMOR: 0
This dinosaur had no body armor, but its bulk would have protected it from most other creatures.

SPEED: 2
Plateosaurus was not a fast-moving animal. It usually lumbered along on all fours.

AGILITY: 5
Although it was not an agile creature, Plateosaurus was skilled at using its long tail to help balance its body when it stood on its two back legs to feed.

SCARINESS: 8
When it reared up to its full height, Plateosaurus would have been an awe-inspiring animal, capable of scaring off many would-be predators.

SPECIAL SKILLS: 8
Plateosaurus was an expert grazer: it had lots of tiny leaf-shaped teeth and strong jaw muscles for nibbling at plants.

EORAPTOR VS. HERRERASAURUS

THE BATTLE
TIME:
Late Triassic
PLACE:
South America: Argentina
WINNER:
Herrerasaurus

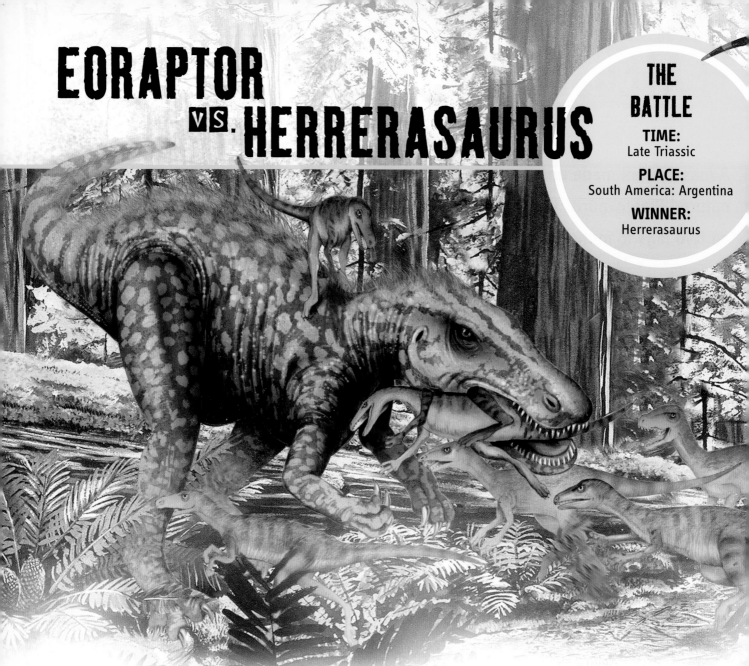

Desperate for food, a pack of sharp-toothed Eoraptors have attacked the much larger Herrerasaurus. Together they snap and claw at the other animal's legs and arms, but he is just too strong for them. Herrerasaurus manages to snap up one or two Eoraptors in his powerful jaws before the pack give up their attack and run for safety.

Competitor ① EORAPTOR

Order: Therapoda
Family: Eoraptoridae
Size: 3 ft (90 cm) long

Eoraptor was one of the earliest known dinosaurs. Like its relative Herrerasaurus, it was a fast-moving carnivore and had sharp teeth for attacking its prey.

Competitor ② HERRERASAURUS

Order: Saurischia
Family: Herrerasauridae
Size: 10 ft (3 m) long

Herrerasaurus was much larger and more heavily built than Eoraptor. It had a long head with particularly flexible jaws so it could bite more efficiently. Its fingers were long and strong with sharp, curved claws for seizing prey.

HYPSOGNATHUS
aka SPIKY

In the Late Triassic there were many small reptiles such as Hypsognathus scurrying around, searching for food to eat. Hypsognathus ate plants, but many of its relatives were insect-eaters.

BONUS FEATURE:
HEAD SPIKES

The sharp spikes on either side of its broad head helped protect the otherwise defenseless little Hypsognathus from predators.

VITAL STATISTICS
Order: Procolophonia
Family: Procolophonidae
Period: Late Triassic
Home territory: North America: New Jersey
Habitat: Dry plains
Size: 1 ft (30 cm) long

DISTINGUISHING FEATURES
This small lizardlike reptile had a short, stout body and sprawling legs. It probably ate plants, which it chewed with its broad teeth.

COMBAT HISTORY
Meat-eating dinosaurs such as Coelophysis would have snapped up something the size of Hypsognathus, but this little reptile's spiky head may have put off some predators.

STRENGTH: 2
Hypsognathus was powerfully built for its size but not very strong.

ARMOR: 5
Although it had no body armor, this early reptile had a frightening array of spikes around its head.

SPEED: 1
Hypsognathus probably had little need for speed as it crawled around feeding on plants.

AGILITY: 1
With its squat body and short legs, Hypsognathus would not have been very agile.

SCARINESS: 4
For its size, spiky Hypsognathus had a surprisingly fierce appearance.

SPECIAL SKILLS: 5
It may not be all that exciting, but Hypsognathus was perfectly suited to its life as a ground-living plant-eater.

PROGANOCHELYS
aka SLOW COACH

One of the earliest turtles, Proganochelys lived more than 200 million years ago but looked amazingly like turtles today. Like them, Proganochelys had a hard shell to protect itself from enemies.

BONUS FEATURE:
THE SHELL
This turtle's broad, domed shell covered its back, while extra bony plates round the edges protected its legs.

VITAL STATISTICS
Order: Testudines
Family: Proganochelyidae
Period: Late Triassic
Home territory: Europe
Habitat: Rivers and lakes
Size: 3 ft (90 cm) long

DISTINGUISHING FEATURES
Like turtles today, Proganochelys had a toothless horn-covered beak that it used to snap up plants, but it did also have some small teeth.

COMBAT HISTORY
Cowardly Proganochelys was not a fighter and would have depended on its tough shell to defend itself. But unlike turtles today, it could not pull its head right into its shell.

STRENGTH: 2
Proganochelys's hard shell would have made up for its lack of strength.

ARMOR: 8
Proganochelys's tough shell was covered with plates of smooth horn, or tortoiseshell, making it even stronger. More hard plates protected the turtle's soft underside.

SPEED: 1
With its broad body and short legs, Proganochelys would have paddled slowly through the water.

AGILITY: 1
Its shell makes it hard for a turtle to be agile, as it cannot bend or maneuver its body very easily.

SCARINESS: 1
With teeth only just sharp enough to munch on plants, this turtle was more easily scared than scary!

SPECIAL SKILLS: 4
Slow-moving, peace-loving Proganochelys would have had to be an expert at avoiding confrontations with the other water-dwelling inhabitants of Triassic Europe.

JURASSIC

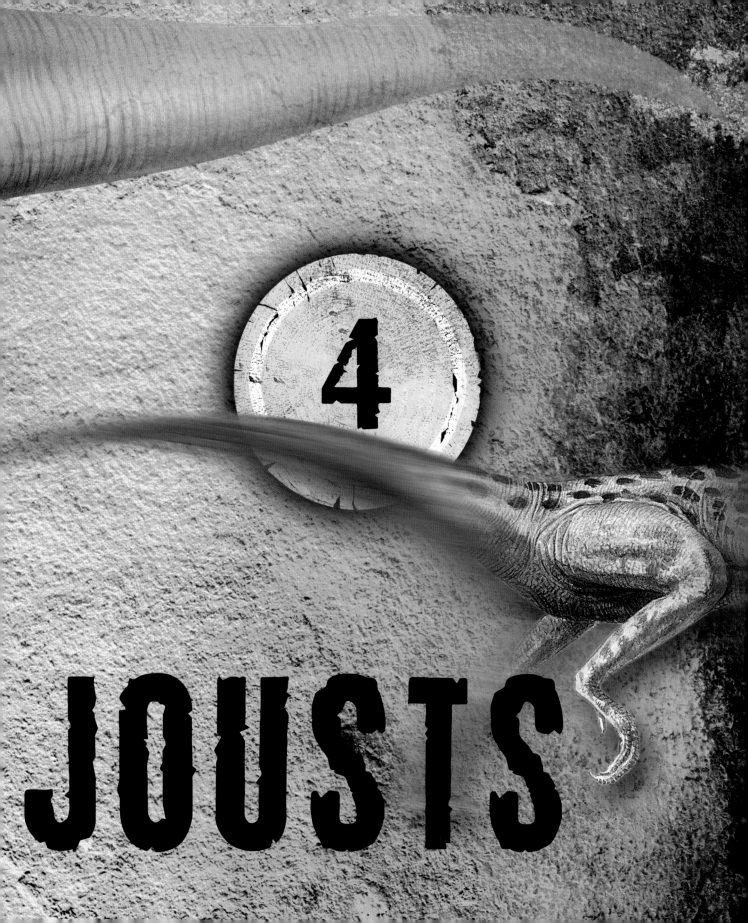

4

JOUSTS

COMBAT ZONE: THE JURASSIC PERIOD

Shunosaurus,
a sauropod

Ginkgo

Angustinaripterus,
a flying reptile
(pterosaur)

Gasosaurus,
a tetanuran

Conifer

Huayangosaurus,
a stegosaur

Tree ferns

During the Jurassic, the world's climate was much warmer than it is now and there was lots of rain. These conditions were ideal for plant life, and large, dense forests of ferns, conifers, and ginkgos grew over much of the land.

⬆ THE JURASSIC LANDSCAPE

In this Jurassic landscape in what is now southwest China, a pack of fierce Gasosaurus dinosaurs are about to attack a feeding stegosaur. Peaceful sauropods look up in alarm—even they could be in danger from these sharp-toothed predators.

So many plants meant plenty of food for plant-eaters, and more and more kinds of plant-eating dinosaurs evolved and flourished. These included huge sauropods, the biggest creatures that have ever lived on land. A sauropod could munch its way through more than 1 ton of plants a day. Many different kinds of meat-eating dinosaurs thrived too, as they had lots of prey to choose from. Powerful killers such as Allosaurus, Megalosaurus, and Gasosaurus prowled the forests, attacking anything that crossed their path.

In the air were more kinds of pterosaurs than ever before, and the very first birds, such as Archaeopteryx, appeared. The oceans, too, were full of life. The most powerful hunters were still marine reptiles, such as ichthyosaurs and plesiosaurs. They preyed on the many kinds of fish in Jurassic seas as well as on creatures such as ammonites and belemnites, relatives of today's squid and octopus.

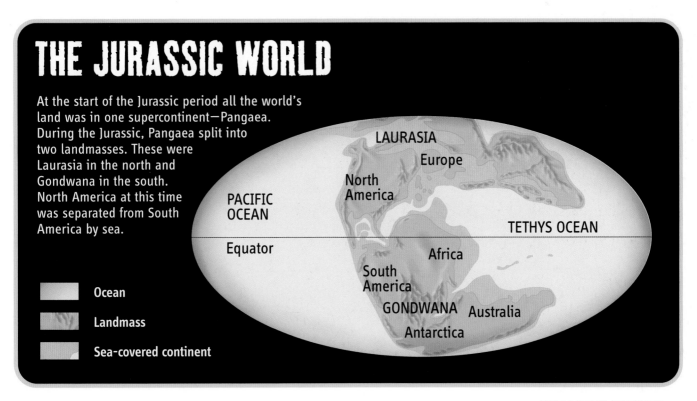

THE JURASSIC WORLD

At the start of the Jurassic period all the world's land was in one supercontinent—Pangaea. During the Jurassic, Pangaea split into two landmasses. These were Laurasia in the north and Gondwana in the south. North America at this time was separated from South America by sea.

LAURASIA

Europe

North America

PACIFIC OCEAN

TETHYS OCEAN

Equator

Africa

South America

GONDWANA Australia

Antarctica

Ocean

Landmass

Sea-covered continent

TELEOSAURUS

aka TRAPPER

A fast-swimming killer, Teleosaurus could live on land but was most at home in the sea. It chased prey such as fish and squid, snapping them up with ease.

VITAL STATISTICS

Order: Crocodylia
Family: Teleosauridae
Period: Early Jurassic
Home territory: Europe
Habitat: The oceans
Size: 10 ft (3 m) long

DISTINGUISHING FEATURES

This early crocodile had extremely long slender jaws lined with lots of sharp teeth—ideal for catching fish.

COMBAT HISTORY

In Jurassic times, as now, crocodiles were among the most dangerous of all predators. Few creatures dared to attack these aggressive, heavily armored reptiles.

STRENGTH: 8

Teleosaurus had a strong, muscular body and powerful jaws that snapped shut on its prey.

ARMOR: 8

Like crocodiles today, Teleosaurus's back was heavily armored with plates of bone set into its tough skin.

SPEED: 7

Teleosaurus swam swiftly through the water by movements of its long body and tail. It held its short front legs against its body and paddled with its longer back legs.

AGILITY: 6

On land, this reptile scurried along on all four legs, but couldn't move as fast, or with such agility, as it could in water.

SCARINESS: 7

Teleosaurus was a fearsome hunter and an expert underwater predator.

SPECIAL SKILLS: 8

Teleosaurus's sharp teeth interlocked when its mouth snapped shut, trapping any prey inside.

SCUTELLOSAURUS

aka STUDS

This little dinosaur was an early type of stegosaur. A peaceful plant-eater, it needed its body armor to protect it from the many predators that prowled Jurassic forests.

VITAL STATISTICS
Order: Ornithischia
Family: Scelidosauridae
Period: Early Jurassic
Home territory: Western North America
Habitat: Forest
Size: 4 ft (1.2 m)

DISTINGUISHING FEATURES
Scutellosaurus had an extremely long tail, about half its total body length.

COMBAT HISTORY
As it nibbled plants in the forests of North America, Scutellosaurus was always on the alert for strong-clawed hunters such as Dilophosaurus, which ripped its prey apart with its powerful hands.

STRENGTH: 1
This weedy dinosaur was not very strong and could not fight off attackers.

ARMOR: 6
Hundreds of sharp-edged studs covered this dinosaur's back and sides, and gave some protection from the sharp jaws of its enemies.

SPEED: 6
Scutellosaurus could probably run fast on its back legs as well as walk on all fours.

AGILITY: 1
When running fast, Scutellosaurus held its long tail out behind it to balance the weight of the front of its body.

SCARINESS: 0
Scutellosaurus was too small to strike fear into anything!

SPECIAL SKILLS: 2
This timid fellow did its best to escape from danger. If cornered it had no weapons to defend itself and relied on its bony body armor.

SPECIAL SKILL: SWIMMING

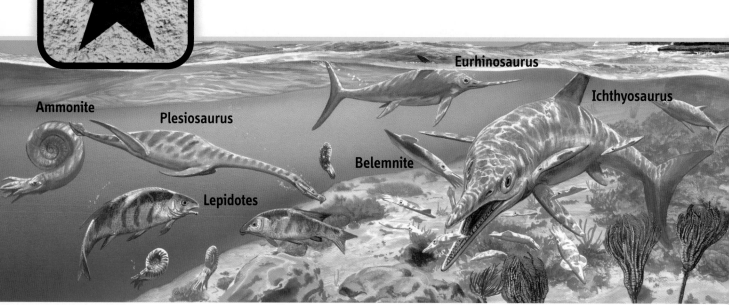

Ammonite

Plesiosaurus

Eurhinosaurus

Ichthyosaurus

Belemnite

Lepidotes

Jaws open, ready to snatch its prey, an ichthyosaur pursues a shoal of belemnites, relatives of today's octopus and squid. Other ichthyosaurs and a plesiosaur arrive, ready to snap up smaller sea creatures as they scatter in alarm.

While dinosaurs ruled life on land, marine reptiles dominated the Jurassic oceans. Biggest and most successful of these were plesiosaurs and ichthyosaurs. Plesiosaurs had strong bodies, short tails, and long flippers. They fed on fish and squid and spent nearly all their lives in the water. However, just like turtles today, once a year plesiosaurs came out onto land to lay their eggs.

Ichthyosaurs were even better adapted to life in the sea. A typical ichthyosaur had a sleek, streamlined body with a strong tail that helped propel it through the water. Like dolphins today, they cruised the oceans at high speed, hunting any prey that came their way—mostly fish and squid. They did not come to land to lay eggs, but gave birth to their young in the water.

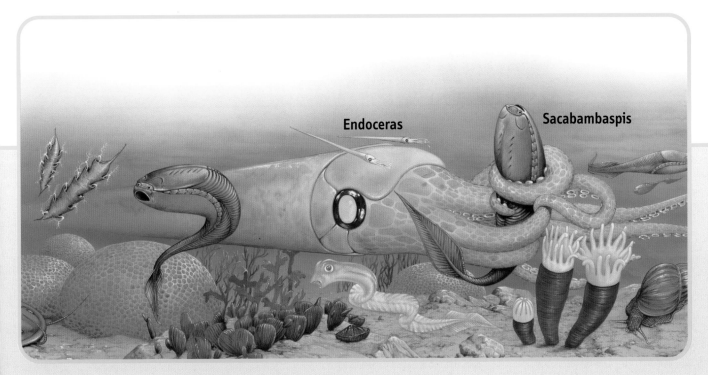

Endoceras

Sacabambaspis

Fish were plentiful in Jurassic waters. But the first fishlike creatures lived long before, in Ordovician times, more than 450 million years ago. Toothless, fishlike animals such as Sacabambaspis fell victim to powerful hunters such as Endoceras, a type of early octopus.

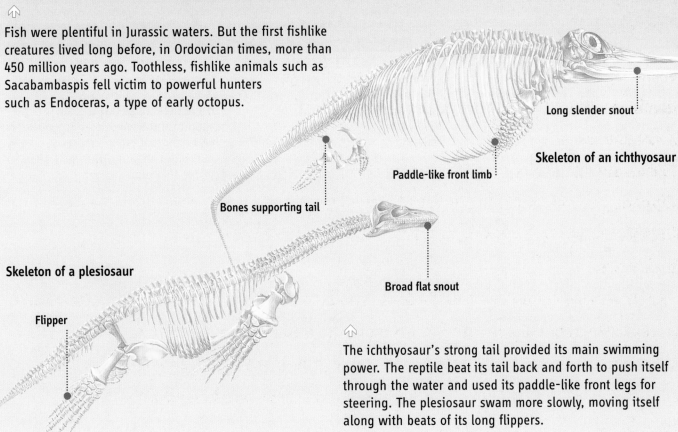

Long slender snout

Skeleton of an ichthyosaur

Paddle-like front limb

Bones supporting tail

Broad flat snout

Skeleton of a plesiosaur

Flipper

The ichthyosaur's strong tail provided its main swimming power. The reptile beat its tail back and forth to push itself through the water and used its paddle-like front legs for steering. The plesiosaur swam more slowly, moving itself along with beats of its long flippers.

LESOTHOSAURUS
aka **SPRINTER**

DANGER LEVEL **3.3**

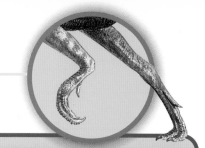

A small, fast-moving dinosaur, Lesothosaurus sped over dry plains, searching for plants to eat. With its sharp pointed teeth, it could munch its way through the toughest leaves and stems.

BONUS FEATURE:
LONG LEGS

Its long, slender back legs made this lightly built dinosaur a very fast runner indeed, able to speed off at the first whiff of danger.

VITAL STATISTICS
Order: Ornithischia
Family: Fabrosauridae
Period: Early Jurassic
Home territory: Southern Africa
Habitat: Hot, dry plains
Size: 3 ft (1 m) long

DISTINGUISHING FEATURES
Lesothosaurus had a small, lizardlike head and jaws lined with sharp teeth shaped like arrowheads. Its front legs were tiny compared to its back legs.

COMBAT HISTORY
With few defenses other than its speed, Lesothosaurus was always on the alert for danger. At the slightest hint of the approach of a predator, such as flesh-eating Ceratosaurus, Lesothosaurus would flee.

STRENGTH: 2
Its light build meant that Lesothosaurus was not strong. However, its most powerful muscles were in its thighs, enabling it to run fast.

ARMOR: 0
This dinosaur had no body armor and no defense against its enemies except its speed.

SPEED: 8
Lesothosaurus moved upright on its two back legs and could run fast—at up to 30 mph (50 km/h).

AGILITY: 8
Like other small, slender dinosaurs, Lesothosaurus was a graceful creature, able to leap and jump with ease.

SCARINESS: 0
This small plant-eater was not big or fierce enough to frighten other creatures.

SPECIAL SKILLS: 2
Lesothosaurus was well equipped for feeding on plants, using its small front legs to pick leaves and stuff them into its mouth.

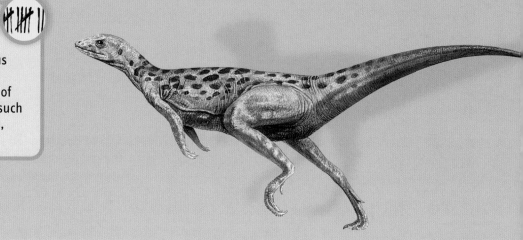

CRYOLOPHOSAURUS
aka THE MASTER

This mighty predator terrorized the plant-eaters of Jurassic Antarctica with its hooklike claws and jagged teeth. It was the first and only flesh-eating dinosaur ever found in Antarctica.

BONUS FEATURE:
THE CREST
On Cryolophosaurus's head was a crest with small horns on each side. It may have shown off this crest in its mating displays.

VITAL STATISTICS
Order: Saurischia
Family: Allosauridae
Period: Early Jurassic
Home territory: Antarctica
Habitat: Near rivers
Size: 23–26 ft (7–8 m) long

DISTINGUISHING FEATURES
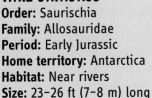
Cryolophosaurus had a bulky body, powerful legs, and massive jaws.

COMBAT HISTORY
Cryolophosaurus had no equals in its Antarctic home—it was the top predator and could kill any plant-eater, such as a prosauropod. While holding its victim in its strong fingers, Cryolophosaurus could slash at its prey's flesh with the deadly claws on its feet.

STRENGTH: 9
An immensely strong animal, Cryolophosaurus was able to overcome anything it attacked.

ARMOR: 0
Cryolophosaurus had no body armor—but didn't really need it. Who would have dared attack this fearsome creature?

SPEED: 7
This dinosaur could run fast but only for short distances, so preferred to creep up on prey.

AGILITY: 8
A powerful tail helped balance the weight of the front of this dinosaur's body, enabling it to run upright on two legs.

SCARINESS: 9
This vicious hunter was the most frightening creature in its home territory—the animal that all others did their best to avoid.

SPECIAL SKILLS: 9
Like other large predators, Cryolophosaurus hunted by a combination of stealth and speed. Having spotted a herd of peaceful plant-eaters, such as prosauropods, it lurked among the trees, waiting for a chance to strike. When the moment came, this assassin made a speedy dash to seize and kill its prey.

THE BATTLE
TIME:
Late Jurassic
PLACE:
Africa
WINNER:
Kentrosaurus escapes

KENTROSAURUS VS. ALLOSAURUS

Although Allosaurus usually hunts in packs, this hungry dinosaur is on its own today and has been watching a herd of Kentrosaurus munching plants. At last, one of the stegosaurs strays away from the herd—and Allosaurus strikes. As soon as Kentrosaurus realizes what's happening, he begins to bellow and pound with his hooves. He lashes out with his heavy tail, which is lined with sharp spikes, cutting deep into his attacker's flesh. Despite her hunger, Allosaurus retreats. She knows the damage this swinging tail can do.

Competitor ①

KENTROSAURUS

Order: Ornithischia
Family: Stegosauridae
Size: 16 ft (5 m) long

Although much smaller than Allosaurus, Kentrosaurus was well armored with vicious bony spikes on its back and tail. A blow of its powerful tail could seriously wound any attacker.

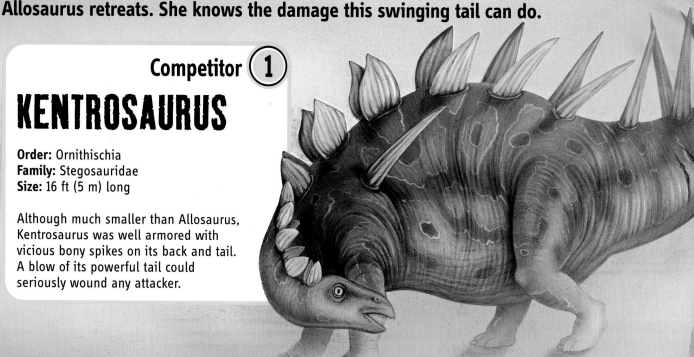

ALLOSAURUS

Order: Saurischia
Family: Allosauridae
Size: 39 ft (12 m) long

Fearsome Allosaurus weighed up to 2 tons and was more than a match for any animal of its time. These killers hunted in packs and even attacked huge sauropods and stegosaurs.

LUFENGOSAURUS
aka THE HEAVY

This large, heavily built reptile was one of the earliest of the giant plant-eating dinosaurs. It could rear up on its strong back legs and feed on leaves high in the trees.

VITAL STATISTICS
Order: Saurischia
Family: Plateosauridae
Period: Early Jurassic
Home territory: Asia: China
Habitat: Open plains and woodland
Size: 16–23 ft (5–7 m) long

DISTINGUISHING FEATURES
Lufengosaurus had a bulky body, front legs shorter than its back legs, and a long, powerful tail. Its neck was long and its head small.

COMBAT HISTORY
Lufengosaurus preferred to mind its own business and stay out of trouble, but if attacked would not give up without a fight. A blow of its mighty tail and a slash of its sharp claws were enough to put off many predators, such as Gasosaurus.

⚒ STRENGTH: 8
Lufengosaurus was a strong, muscular animal, capable of defending itself against attackers.

🛡 ARMOR: 3
This dinosaur had no body armor but could lash out with its massive tail.

⏱ SPEED: 6
Although Lufengosaurus was not a speedy dinosaur, it could walk on its two back legs as well as on all fours.

⚡ AGILITY: 6
Lufengosaurus's bulky tail helped balance its body when it stood up on two legs.

☠ SCARINESS: 9
Sheer size made Lufengosaurus an awesome sight. This dinosaur was almost as long as two cars parked end to end.

★ SPECIAL SKILLS: 3
Lufengosaurus fed by stripping leaves from the trees with its jagged-edged teeth. Its strong claws were useful for gathering food—and for defending itself against attackers.

LEXOVISAURUS
aka PRICKLE

Like all stegosaurs, Lexovisaurus was a plant-eater. This large bulky-bodied dinosaur wandered the forests, searching for food and doing its best to stay out of trouble.

VITAL STATISTICS
Order: Ornithischia
Family: Stegosauridae
Period: Middle Jurassic
Home territory: Europe
Habitat: Forests
Size: 16 ft (5 m) long

DISTINGUISHING FEATURES
This stegosaur had a pair of spines measuring up to 4 feet (1.2 meters) long jutting out from its shoulders, as well as 12 spines on its tail.

COMBAT HISTORY
With its spikes and bony armor, Lexovisaurus was a dangerous prospect for any predator. Only the largest flesh-eating dinosaurs, such as Megalosaurus, would dare attack stegosaurs.

STRENGTH: 8
A powerfully well-built animal, Lexovisaurus was big and strong enough to defend itself against most attackers.

ARMOR: 8
Lexovisaurus was a formidably well-armored dinosaur. As well as the spines on its shoulders and tail, it had bony plates lining its back and neck.

SPEED: 6
For a bulky animal, Lexovisaurus could gallop along at surprising speed to escape from danger.

AGILITY: 1
A typical stegosaur with a heavy tail and trunklike legs, Lexovisaurus was a lumbering creature.

SCARINESS: 6
A pair of 4-foot (1.2-meter) spikes makes any animal look fearsome—and Lexovisaurus was no exception!

SPECIAL SKILLS: 5
When cornered, this stegosaur would lash out with its spiky tail and could seriously wound an attacker.

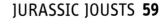

STEGOSAURUS
aka THE TANK

Stegosaurus was the biggest of the stegosaurs and, like all of its kind, it was a large, slow-moving plant-eater. This animal was longer than an African elephant and weighed as much as 2 tons.

BONUS FEATURE:
TAIL SPIKES
At the end of Stegosaurus's tail were some very useful defensive weapons—two pairs of formidably sharp spikes.

DISTINGUISHING FEATURES
This dinosaur's huge body was topped with two rows of large bony plates, arranged in alternating rows. The largest of these plates were 15 inches (40 cm) tall. Scientists think the plates may have helped stegosaurs control their body temperature. The plates were covered with blood-rich skin. When the animal was cold, it turned toward the sun so the heat warmed the blood as it passed over the plates. If the stegosaur was hot, it turned away from the sun and into the breeze so the plates gave off heat and cooled the animal down.

VITAL STATISTICS
Order: Ornithischia
Family: Stegosauridae
Period: Late Jurassic
Home territory: North America
Habitat: Woodland
Size: 30 ft (9 m) long

COMBAT HISTORY
A Stegosaurus was not an easy opponent. When threatened by a predatory dinosaur such as Allosaurus, Stegosaurus stood its ground and lashed out with its strong, spiked tail, while pounding its feet and roaring. Not surprisingly, many predators did not stay around to see what happened next.

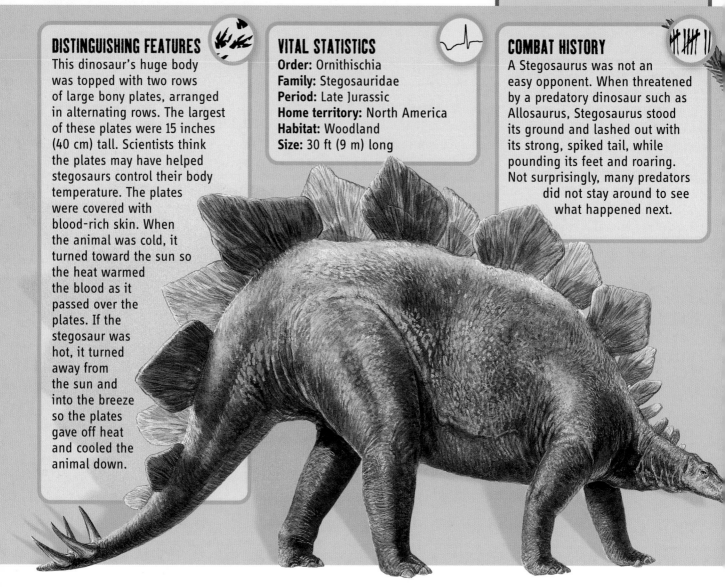

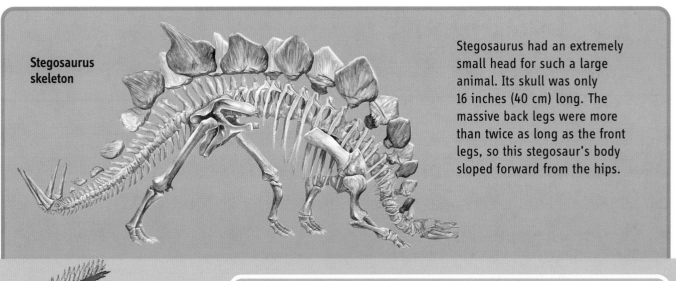

Stegosaurus skeleton

Stegosaurus had an extremely small head for such a large animal. Its skull was only 16 inches (40 cm) long. The massive back legs were more than twice as long as the front legs, so this stegosaur's body sloped forward from the hips.

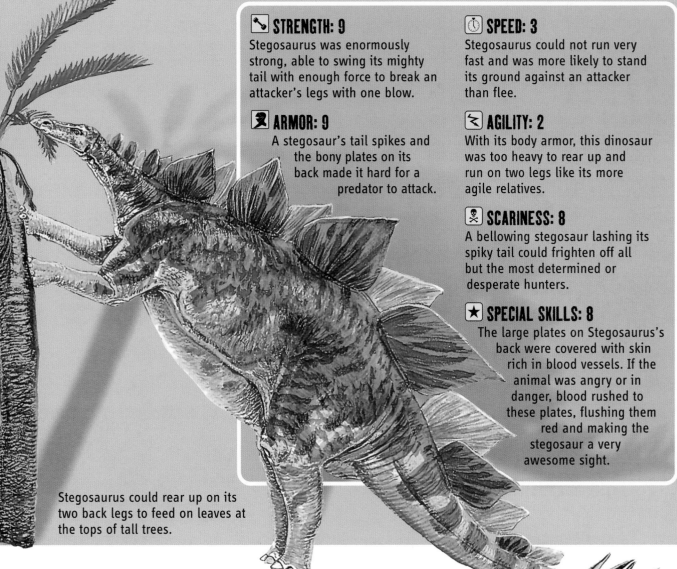

🔧 STRENGTH: 9
Stegosaurus was enormously strong, able to swing its mighty tail with enough force to break an attacker's legs with one blow.

🏃 ARMOR: 9
A stegosaur's tail spikes and the bony plates on its back made it hard for a predator to attack.

⏱ SPEED: 3
Stegosaurus could not run very fast and was more likely to stand its ground against an attacker than flee.

〰 AGILITY: 2
With its body armor, this dinosaur was too heavy to rear up and run on two legs like its more agile relatives.

☠ SCARINESS: 8
A bellowing stegosaur lashing its spiky tail could frighten off all but the most determined or desperate hunters.

★ SPECIAL SKILLS: 8
The large plates on Stegosaurus's back were covered with skin rich in blood vessels. If the animal was angry or in danger, blood rushed to these plates, flushing them red and making the stegosaur a very awesome sight.

Stegosaurus could rear up on its two back legs to feed on leaves at the tops of tall trees.

MAMENCHISAURUS
aka THE TALL GUY

This giant plant-eating dinosaur had the longest neck of any animal that has ever lived. It made up about half of the dinosaur's total length and contained 19 very long vertebrae to support it.

BONUS FEATURE:
THE NECK
The amazingly long neck of this dino enabled it to reach leaves at the tops of trees. Standing on its hind legs gave a yet greater reach.

VITAL STATISTICS
Order: Saurischia
Family: Diplodocidae
Period: Late Jurassic
Home territory: Asia: Mongolia
Habitat: Woodlands near water
Size: 72 ft (22 m) long from nose to tail

DISTINGUISHING FEATURES
At the end of its extraordinary neck, Mamenchisaurus had a very small head. Its bulky body was supported by strong, pillarlike legs, and it had a very long tail.

COMBAT HISTORY
Mamenchisaurus probably lived in herds, keeping their young close to them to protect them from predators. Only the largest flesh-eating dinosaurs, such as Yangchuanosaurus, would dare attack these long-necked giants—and even they were often sent packing.

STRENGTH: 9
An animal this size had to be very strong just to move around—and Mamenchisaurus was no exception. It had powerful back muscles that it used to lash its tail back and forth. However, this dinosaur's long neck was vulnerable to attack.

ARMOR: 0
Like most sauropod dinosaurs, Mamenchisaurus had no body armor and depended on its size for protection from enemies.

SPEED: 6
Mamenchisaurus walked along with giant strides but was not a particularly fast mover. It walked on all fours but could rear up on two legs to reach food high in the trees.

AGILITY: 2
As it walked, this dinosaur held its long neck straight out in front, which restricted its movements.

SCARINESS: 10
An animal the size of a bus cannot fail to be frightening, even though it only fed on leaves and preferred to avoid conflict.

SPECIAL SKILLS: 9
If attacked, Mamenchisaurus could fight back with its long whiplike tail. One lash of this could stun an enemy. This dinosaur could also rear up on its back legs and pound an attacker with its front legs.

PTERODAUSTRO
aka THE SIEVE

A pterosaur about the size of today's eagle, Pterodaustro soared over the oceans on its strong, yet delicate wings, searching for food to eat. Swooping down, it used its amazing jaws to scoop small prey from the water.

BONUS FEATURE:
THE JAWS
Pterodaustro's long jaws were lined with hundreds of slender teeth that formed a comblike sieve to filter small prey.

VITAL STATISTICS
Order: Pterosauria
Family: Pterodaustridae
Period: Late Jurassic
Home territory: South America: Argentina
Habitat: The sea and coastlines
Size: 4 ft (1.2 m) from wingtip to wingtip

DISTINGUISHING FEATURES
Pterodaustro's extraordinary jaws curved upward at the tip, ideal for scooping up prey.

COMBAT HISTORY
Pterdaustro had no defenses—only its ability to fly. Fortunately there were few airborne predators in Jurassic times, and this pterosaur would only have been in danger if attacked on land.

STRENGTH: 3
Winged reptiles such as Pterodaustro had very little strength. Only its long jaws were powerful.

ARMOR: 0
Pterodaustro had no body armor to protect it, but could fly to escape from danger.

SPEED: 8
Pterodaustro was a fast flier, able to use both flapping and soaring flight as it traveled over water looking for food.

AGILITY: 5
Like all pterosaurs, Pterodaustro was less agile on land than in the air. It scuttled about on all fours, using the claws on its wings as well as its feet.

SCARINESS: 0
Pterodaustro fed only on microscopic prey and was not a frightening hunter.

SPECIAL SKILLS: 6
Pterodaustro used its specialized jaws to filter its food from the sea. It scooped up a mouthful of tiny animals, water, and mud. As it closed its jaws, its bristle-like teeth formed a sieve, trapping any prey as the water drained away. Pterodaustro then gulped down its meal.

BATTLE TACTIC: **SPEED**

Dromaeosaurus chased its prey at high speed.

When close to its victim, it pounced toward it.

Leaping up off the ground, it tore at the animal's flesh with its claws.

Not all dinosaurs were hefty monsters with horns and body armor. For some of the smaller dinosaurs, speed was a vital tactic for catching prey.

One of the secrets of the dinosaurs' success was that they moved more efficiently and more quickly than earlier reptiles. Creatures before them walked like most lizards do today, with their legs sprawled out to the sides. A dinosaur's legs were held straight down under the body, which meant they could carry more weight and take longer, faster strides. Dinosaurs also had long tails. Many used their tail to balance the weight of the front of the body, allowing them to run on their hind legs.

⬇ Dromaeosaurus ran very fast on its hind legs, reaching speeds of 37 mph (60 km/h). On each hand were three sharp-clawed fingers that it used to seize its prey.

The fastest dinosaurs were slender, birdlike creatures such as Ornithomimus, Gallimimus, and Struthiomimus. They had very long hind limbs with big powerful thigh muscles that allowed them to run fast and speed away from danger.

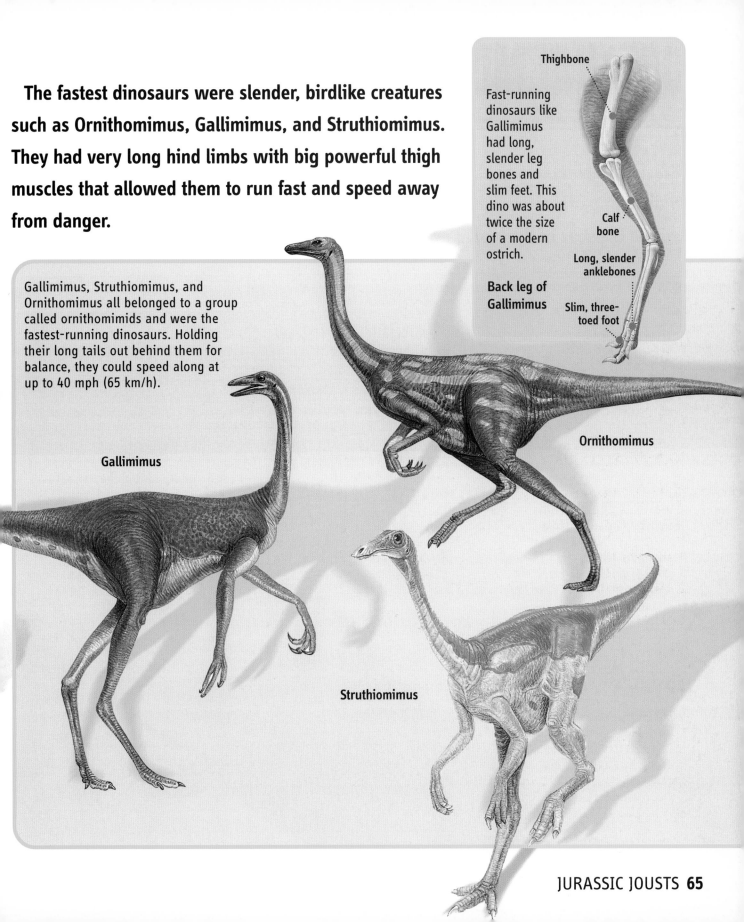

Fast-running dinosaurs like Gallimimus had long, slender leg bones and slim feet. This dino was about twice the size of a modern ostrich.

Thighbone

Calf bone

Long, slender anklebones

Slim, three-toed foot

Back leg of Gallimimus

Gallimimus, Struthiomimus, and Ornithomimus all belonged to a group called ornithomimids and were the fastest-running dinosaurs. Holding their long tails out behind them for balance, they could speed along at up to 40 mph (65 km/h).

Gallimimus

Ornithomimus

Struthiomimus

OPHTHALMOSAURUS

aka WATCHER

DANGER LEVEL 5.2

A fast-swimming hunter, Ophthalmosaurus belonged to the group of marine reptiles called ichthyosaurs. It cruised the seas of the world, preying on fish and squid.

BONUS FEATURE:

THE EYES

This ichthyosaur's huge eyes, up to 4 inches (10 cm) across, helped it hunt in the dark, deep seas.

VITAL STATISTICS

Order: Ichthyosauria
Family: Ichthyosauridae
Period: Late Jurassic
Home territory: Europe, western North America, South America
Habitat: The oceans
Size: 11 ft 6 in (3.5 m) long

DISTINGUISHING FEATURES

Ophthalmosaurus had a sleek, streamlined body, about the length of an average-size car, and a large crescent-shaped tail. Its jaws were long and beaklike.

COMBAT HISTORY

Ophthalmosaurus was no match for the largest ocean predators—plesiosaurs such as Liopleurodon. That 80-foot (25-meter) monster could kill an ichthyosaur with one snap of its huge, sharp-toothed jaws.

STRENGTH: 7

This ichthyosaur had powerful muscles and a strong body.

ARMOR: 1

Ophthalmosaurus had no body armor, but a thick layer of fatty blubber gave it some protection.

SPEED: 8

Ophthalmosaurus could speed through the sea at up to 25 mph (40 km/h). Its tail provided the main swimming power.

AGILITY: 8

Like all ichthyosaurs, Ophthalmosaurus was an agile swimmer, using its paddle-shaped flippers to steer as it twisted and turned in pursuit of prey.

SCARINESS: 1

Although it was an expert hunter of fish and squid, Ophthalmosaurus was not fierce or frightening. Its long jaws were toothless, and it swallowed prey whole.

SPECIAL SKILLS: 6

Thanks to its extra-large eyes, this reptile could see well in the dark and was able to track prey in deeper waters than other ichthyosaurs.

TUOJIANGOSAURUS
aka STINGER

This massive, armor-plated dinosaur liked a quiet life and spent most of its time feeding on low-growing plants, such as ferns and cycads.

BONUS FEATURE:
THE TAIL
Sharp spikes at the end of this stegosaur's tail could wound even the biggest attacker.

VITAL STATISTICS
Order: Ornithischia
Family: Stegosauridae
Period: Late Jurassic
Home territory: Asia: China
Habitat: Woodland
Size: 23 ft (7 m) long

DISTINGUISHING FEATURES
A typical stegosaur, Tuojiangosaurus had a tiny head and a deep, bulky body. Fifteen pairs of bony plates lined its huge back.

COMBAT HISTORY
Tuojiangosaurus was slow to rouse and preferred to avoid conflict. But if attacked by a giant flesh-eater such as Yangchuanosaurus, the stegosaur would stand its ground and do its best to defend itself.

STRENGTH: 8
Tuojiangosaurus was enormously strong and its powerful muscles could drive the spikes on its tail into any attacker.

ARMOR: 9
An array of bony plates and sharp spikes protected this stegosaur from the claws and teeth of flesh-eating dinosaurs.

SPEED: 1
This bulky monster could not move fast and had no hope of running away from danger.

AGILITY: 5
Despite its bulk, Tuojiangosaurus could turn its body quickly in order to use its spiked tail as a weapon.

SCARINESS: 8
When angered, a bellowing, tail-lashing Tuojiangosaurus was a frightening sight for all but the largest predators.

SPECIAL SKILLS: 6
The skin covering its bony plates would flush deep red when this stegosaur was angry or frightened. This helped to make it look bigger and more daunting to a predator.

DIPLODOCUS
aka THE HOLLOW

DANGER LEVEL **6**

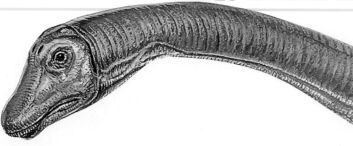

BONUS FEATURE:
THE BENDY NECK
This dinosaur's amazing neck was about 23 feet (7 m) long and contained 15 vertebrae.

Even for a dinosaur, Diplodocus was enormous, one of the largest animals that has ever lived. Longer than a line of seven average cars, this huge reptile weighed more than three African elephants.

COMBAT HISTORY
Diplodocus usually lived in herds. Young animals were in danger from a number of predatory dinosaurs, but the only hunter strong enough to attack and kill a full-grown Diplodocus was the huge flesh-eater Allosaurus. Together, a pack of these hungry killers could tear at a Diplodocus with their sharp claws and teeth.

VITAL STATISTICS
Order: Saurischia
Family: Diplodocidae
Period: Late Jurassic
Home territory: North America
Habitat: Open plains
Size: 85 ft (26 m) long

DISTINGUISHING FEATURES
Diplodocus had a huge body but a tiny head for its size. At just over 24 inches (60 cm) long, its head was not much bigger than the head of today's horse.

STRENGTH: 10
Just moving its own bulk demanded immense strength, so this dinosaur had extraordinarily powerful muscles.

ARMOR: 0
Although Diplodocus had no bony plates or spikes on its body, its huge size was protection enough from all but the fiercest and most foolhardy predators.

SPEED: 2
Diplodocus was not a fast mover—its massive pillarlike legs were designed to support its great bulk, not for speed. The dinosaur ambled along at about 4 mph (6 km/h), not much faster than most humans.

AGILITY: 5
Despite its huge bulk, Diplodocus could rear up on its back legs to feed on high plants, using its strong tail as support.

SCARINESS: 10
Although this leaf-eating giant was not an aggressive animal, its size made it a terrifying sight for smaller dinosaurs.

SPECIAL SKILLS: 9
Powerful muscles enabled Diplodocus to pound its hooves and lash its huge tail from side to side. This dramatic display would be enough to frighten away most predators.

Different types of plant-eating dinosaurs could feed together without getting in one another's way. Long-necked Diplodocus munched the very highest leaves, while smaller horned dinosaurs and hadrosaurs fed on lower-growing plants.

The special structure of this dinosaur's vertebrae (the bones making up its backbone) made Diplodocus light for its size. The bones were partly hollow so they weighed much less than if they were made of solid bone.

APATOSAURUS

aka CRUSHER

DANGER LEVEL **6.3**

Although not as long as Diplodocus, this giant sauropod was far heavier. It weighed an incredible 30 tons, more than six large elephants!

VITAL STATISTICS
Order: Saurischia
Family: Diplodocidae
Period: Late Jurassic
Home territory: Western North America
Habitat: The plains
Size: 70 ft (21 m) long

DISTINGUISHING FEATURES
Apatosaurus had a massive body, long neck, and very long tail. Its head was tiny—only 24 inches (60 cm) long—and its legs were like huge pillars.

COMBAT HISTORY
Only giant flesh-eaters such as Allosaurus dared to attack a mighty Apatosaurus, but they ran the risk of being crushed under its enormous weight or having their bones broken by a lash of its whiplike tail.

STRENGTH: 10
Just moving its body around demanded great strength. This reptile had large, powerful muscles.

ARMOR: 0
An animal of this size didn't really need body armor—its bulk was protection enough.

SPEED: 3
Like Diplodocus, this dinosaur had legs built for strength, not speed, but it had no need to move fast.

SCARINESS: 10
Apatosaurus was originally called Brontosaurus, which means "thunder lizard." The thundering sound of this monster striding across the plains would have terrified most other creatures of the time.

AGILITY: 5
Apatosaurus could stand up on its back legs, but because of its weight this was difficult and a huge effort.

SPECIAL SKILLS: 10
If under attack, this gigantic dinosaur could rear up on its back legs and bring its front legs down to crush its enemy.

RHAMPHORHYNCHUS

aka **WINGS**

DANGER LEVEL **3.3**

Rhamphorhynchus were the earliest, most primitive pterosaurs. They had short legs and a long, bony tail that made up about half the animal's length.

VITAL STATISTICS

Order: Pterosauria
Family: Rhamphorhynchidae
Period: Late Jurassic
Home territory: Europe, Africa
Habitat: The coasts
Size: 3 ft 3 in (1 m) from wingtip to wingtip

DISTINGUISHING FEATURES

This pterosaur had a short neck and large head. Its long jaws were filled with sharp teeth for catching and eating fish.

COMBAT HISTORY

Pterosaurs were not fighters. In the air they were generally safe, but on land they were more at risk. Flesh-eating dinosaurs such as Camptosaurus could easily snap up pterosaurs as they scurried along on land, particularly young animals who were not yet able to fly.

STRENGTH: 3

Pterosaurs like Rhamphorhynchus were strong fliers with powerful wing muscles, but had little strength in their bodies.

ARMOR: 0

Flying reptiles had no body armor. They relied on their ability to fly to escape from danger.

SPEED: 5

Rhamphorhynchus was an expert in the air and could use its broad wings for soaring and for flapping flight, but it was not particularly fast.

AGILITY: 7

The diamond-shaped flap at the end of Rhamphorhynchus's tail acted like a rudder, to help the pterosaur twist and turn with ease as it chased prey.

SCARINESS: 1

A sharp-toothed Rhamphorhynchus might have scared a fish, but not much else.

SPECIAL SKILLS: 6

Rhamphorhynchus could fly just above the sea, dragging its beak in the surface waters. If it came across a fish, the pterosaur snapped its jaws shut, trapping the prey.

THE BATTLE

TIME:
Late Jurassic

PLACE:
North America

WINNER:
Ceratosaurus

BRACHIOSAURUS VS. CERATOSAURUS

A herd of Brachiosaurus is feeding in the afternoon sun. A lively youngster decides to explore and moves away from the herd. A big mistake. A pack of Ceratosaurus have been watching nearby—they pounce, clawing and biting at the Brachiosaurus's tough skin. The sauropod struggles bravely, lashing his tail and roaring. But his wounds are too deep and he soon dies. The Ceratosaurus enjoy their feast.

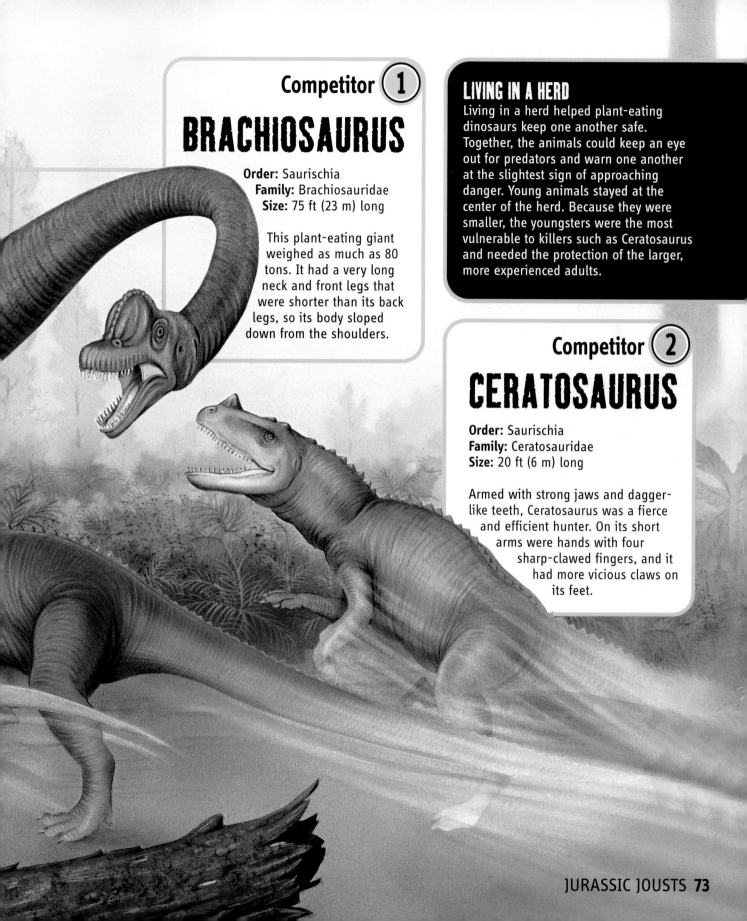

Competitor (1)

BRACHIOSAURUS

Order: Saurischia
Family: Brachiosauridae
Size: 75 ft (23 m) long

This plant-eating giant weighed as much as 80 tons. It had a very long neck and front legs that were shorter than its back legs, so its body sloped down from the shoulders.

LIVING IN A HERD

Living in a herd helped plant-eating dinosaurs keep one another safe. Together, the animals could keep an eye out for predators and warn one another at the slightest sign of approaching danger. Young animals stayed at the center of the herd. Because they were smaller, the youngsters were the most vulnerable to killers such as Ceratosaurus and needed the protection of the larger, more experienced adults.

Competitor (2)

CERATOSAURUS

Order: Saurischia
Family: Ceratosauridae
Size: 20 ft (6 m) long

Armed with strong jaws and dagger-like teeth, Ceratosaurus was a fierce and efficient hunter. On its short arms were hands with four sharp-clawed fingers, and it had more vicious claws on its feet.

SEISMOSAURUS

aka EARTH SHAKER

DANGER LEVEL **6**

This huge plant-eater was one of the biggest creatures that has ever lived. Immensely long and heavy, it would have made the ground tremble beneath its feet as it wandered the Jurassic plains.

VITAL STATISTICS
Order: Saurischia
Family: Diplodocidae
Period: Late Jurassic
Home territory: North America
Habitat: Open plains
Size: 125 ft (38 m) long

DISTINGUISHING FEATURES
Seismosaurus had an enormously long neck and tail, a massive body, and short thick legs to support its bulk. Its head was tiny and it had small teeth only in the front of its jaws.

COMBAT HISTORY
Any predator would have to be very hungry indeed to tackle such a giant. If a pack of ferocious flesh-eaters, such as Allosaurus, were desperate enough to try, Seismosaurus could dispatch them by lashing its mighty whiplike tail from side to side. One blow could shatter a smaller dinosaur's back or legs.

STRENGTH: 10
An animal this size had to be hugely strong, with very powerful muscles, just to move itself around. Its tail alone could inflict damage on a smaller dinosaur.

ARMOR: 0
Like other sauropods, the giant Seismosaurus had no body armor—but who would dare attack anything this size?

SPEED: 3
This sauropod moved slowly on its four short legs. It had no need to rush.

AGILITY: 8
Its long neck was very flexible so Seismosaurus could nose around for food in forests that were too dense for it to walk around in.

SCARINESS: 10
Hearing the footsteps of this earth-shaking giant would have been enough to terrify most animals.

SPECIAL SKILLS: 5
Seismosaurus had teeth that helped it strip leaves from branches but were no good for chewing. Like crocodiles today, it probably swallowed stones that helped grind up the plant food in its stomach.

SCAPHOGNATHUS
aka BRAINY

DANGER LEVEL 3.5

Scientists think that this pterosaur may have had a much larger brain than most reptiles of its size. Perhaps its extra brainpower made it an especially good hunter. Its speedy flight would definitely have given it a head start over its prey.

VITAL STATISTICS
Order: Pterosauria
Family: Rhamphorhynchidae
Period: Late Jurassic
Home territory: Europe
Habitat: Coasts
Size: 3 ft 3 in (1 m) from wingtip to wingtip

DISTINGUISHING FEATURES
Scaphognathus had long jaws lined with sharp teeth, a short neck, and a long bony tail. It was feathered and not much larger than today's crow.

COMBAT HISTORY
Pterosaurs such as Scaphognathus were safe while in the air but more vulnerable on land, where they moved slowly and clumsily. They made an easy mouthful for meat-eating dinosaurs such as Baryonyx.

STRENGTH: 3
Like all pterosaurs, Scaphognathus wasn't very strong, but it had powerful wing muscles. Its wings were made of skin and were strengthened by tough fibers so they weren't easily damaged.

ARMOR: 0
Scaphognathus had no body armor.

SPEED: 7
Pterosaurs were fast fliers, able to soar for long periods over coasts and oceans.

AGILITY: 5
These reptiles were very agile in the air, but scientists aren't sure how they actually took off. They might not have been able to take off from the ground, so instead they may have launched themselves into the air from a cliff or high tree branch.

SCARINESS: 1
Despite its vicious teeth, Scaphognathus was not a frightening creature—unless you were a fish!

SPECIAL SKILLS: 5
Scaphognathus probably used its excellent eyesight to spot prey as it flew low over the sea.

BATTLE TACTIC: STRENGTH

Life-and-death struggles went on between dinosaurs just as they do between animals today. And strength was both an important weapon and a defense.

⬆A giant Cetiosaurus towers over a herd of little Compsognathus in a Jurassic forest. Very few dinosaurs would have dared take on anything with the strength of a sauropod.

TITANOSAURS

Titanosaurs such as Alamosaurus and Saltasaurus were the last group of sauropods to evolve. They first appeared in the Late Jurassic and survived until the end of the Cretaceous period, when all the dinosaurs died out. Like other sauropods, titanosaurs had a long neck and tail, and short, stout legs. They probably ranged from 23 to 100 feet (7–30 meters) in length. Titanosaurs did have one unusual feature: set into the skin were lots of bony plates, some with spikes, that would have helped protect these dinosaurs from meat-eating hunters.

Alamosaurus

All the largest dinosaurs were plant-eaters and they relied on their sheer bulk to protect them. These animals were extremely strong, with heavy bones and powerful muscles. Huge back muscles allowed a sauropod to lash its long tail, which weighed hundreds of pounds, from side to side to best an enemy. If a sauropod reared up on its back legs, it could also bring its full weight down on an attacker—and probably crush it!

The biggest, strongest meat-eating dinosaurs were carnosaurs—creatures such as Tyrannosaurus, Carcharodontosaurus, and Allosaurus. These creatures stood up to 20 feet (6 meters) tall and weighed up to 8 tons—the largest predators that have ever lived on Earth. They were built for power and had massive jaws and daggerlike teeth that could rip an animal apart.

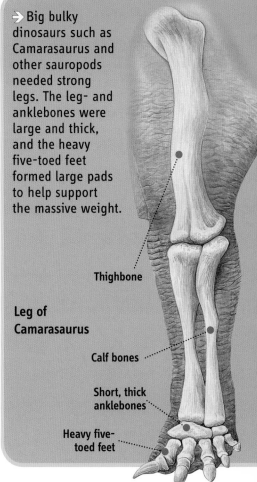

→ Big bulky dinosaurs such as Camarasaurus and other sauropods needed strong legs. The leg- and anklebones were large and thick, and the heavy five-toed feet formed large pads to help support the massive weight.

Thighbone

Leg of Camarasaurus

Calf bones

Short, thick anklebones

Heavy five-toed feet

MEGALOSAURUS

aka BIG GUY

DANGER LEVEL **7.3**

This huge, meat-eating dinosaur was a killer, capable of attacking the great plant-eaters that roamed the same forests. Megalosaurus was the first dinosaur to be scientifically named, in England in 1824.

VITAL STATISTICS

Order: Saurischia
Family: Megalosauridae
Period: Jurassic
Home territory: Europe, Africa
Habitat: Woodland
Size: 30 ft (9 m) long

DISTINGUISHING FEATURES

With its large head, powerful jaws, and curving, serrated teeth, Megalosaurus was well equipped as a hunter and killer.

COMBAT HISTORY

Few creatures would dare attack sauropods, the giant plant-eating dinosaurs which roamed Jurassic forests, but no prey was too big for Megalosaurus to take on. It did not always succeed in killing outright: Its aim was to wound its victim so severely that it was unable to escape or defend itself.

STRENGTH: 9

Megalosaurus was a powerfully muscled animal with a big, strong body and tail, capable of tearing other dinosaurs limb from limb.

ARMOR: 0

This dinosaur had no body armor, but with its collection of weapons it had little need of protection.

SPEED: 8

Megalosaurus walked upright on its strong back legs and could run at speed for short periods when chasing prey. It may have hidden in wait for its prey before swiftly pouncing.

AGILITY: 8

Megalosaurus's heavy tail helped to balance its body as the dinosaur ran and pounced on prey. Walking on two legs allowed this dinosaur to move deftly.

SCARINESS: 10

This killer was one of the scariest creatures of its time and, with its ability to kill dinosaurs twice its size, struck terror into the heart of any plant-eater.

SPECIAL SKILLS: 9

As well as sharp teeth, Megalosaurus had strong clawed fingers and toes, which it used to grasp its prey and tear at its flesh.

FOSSILS

Fossils of dinosaur bones and teeth help dinosaur experts work out what these amazing creatures, such as Megalosaurus, looked like when they were alive. Fossils take a long time to form. When an animal such as a dinosaur dies, much of its flesh is eaten by other animals and insects until only the bones are left. If these bones happen to be lying near a river or lake, they may gradually sink into the mud. Gradually more and more layers of mud pile up over them. Water, carrying minerals, filters down into the ground—and the bones. Slowly these minerals replace the minerals in the bones and turn them into stone. If, millions of years later, some of the land where the fossilized bones lie is worn away by erosion, they may be revealed once again.

1 A dinosaur dies on a lakeshore.
2 The skeleton sinks into the lake.
3 Layers of mud settle over the skeleton, and the bones gradually turn to stone.
4 Erosion removes some of the rock above the fossilized skeleton.
5 As more rock erodes away, the skeleton is revealed.

Megalosaurus lies in wait for its prey, lurking behind trees until an unsuspecting plant-eater comes near enough for the predator to seize it in its large curved fangs.

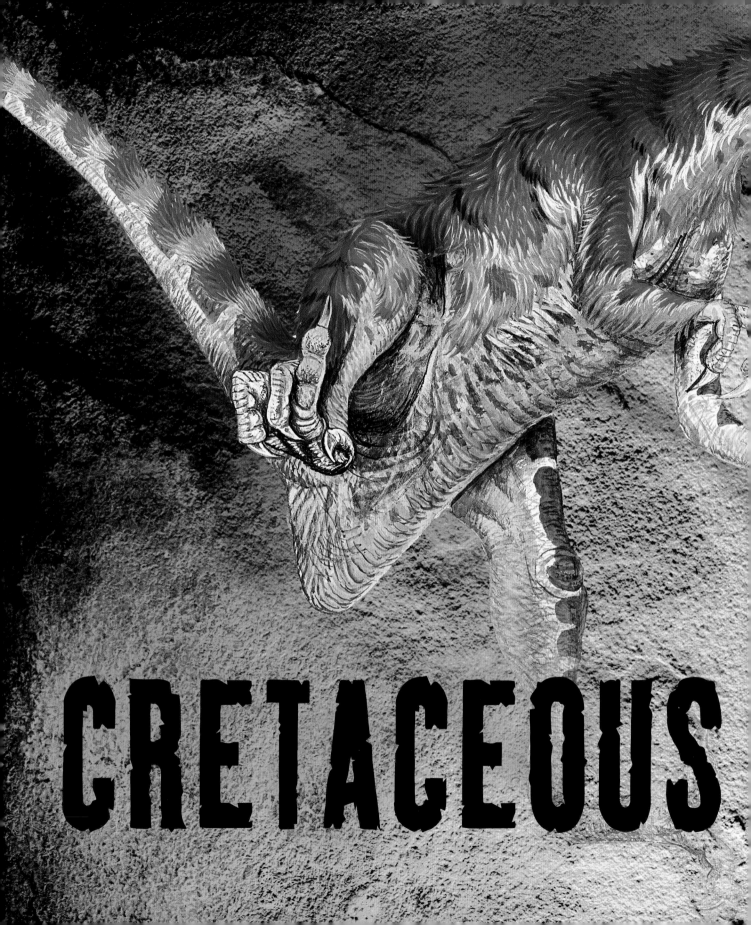

CRETACEOUS

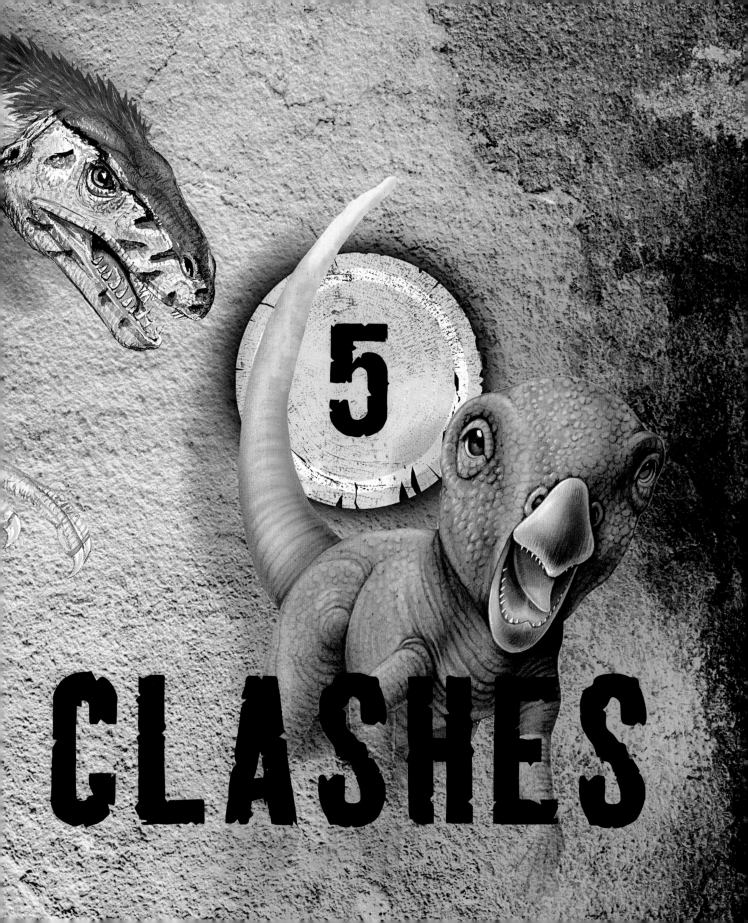

5

CLASHES

Pteranodon

Corythosaurus

Early oystercatcher

Troodon

Corythosaurus

Albertosaurus

Centrosaurus

Troodon

Small mammal

Lizard

The Cretaceous period began 146 million years ago. During this time the climate was generally warm, but there were clear differences between the seasons. The first flowering plants evolved. Deciduous trees, such as oaks and sycamores, flowering bushes, and herbs became more common than horsetails, cycads, and ferns, and covered much of the land.

More plants meant more food for dinosaurs, and many new kinds of dinosaurs, such as horned dinosaurs and duckbills, appeared. Pollinating insects evolved too, and more kinds of mammals and birds, many of which fed on plants and seeds.

But the dinosaurs' days were numbered. At the end of the Cretaceous, some huge catastrophe on Earth, possibly the impact of a giant meteorite, led to the death of the dinosaurs and many other kinds of creatures, including pterosaurs and ichthyosaurs. These amazing reptiles disappeared forever.

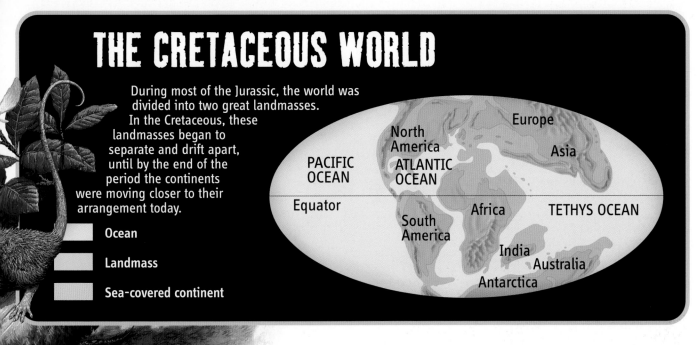

THE CRETACEOUS WORLD

During most of the Jurassic, the world was divided into two great landmasses. In the Cretaceous, these landmasses began to separate and drift apart, until by the end of the period the continents were moving closer to their arrangement today.

- Ocean
- Landmass
- Sea-covered continent

Europe
North America
Asia
PACIFIC OCEAN
ATLANTIC OCEAN
Equator
Africa
TETHYS OCEAN
South America
India
Australia
Antarctica

◄ In this Cretaceous landscape in what is now Montana, USA, Corythosaurus, a plant-eating dinosaur, has returned to her nest to find a fierce little Troodon stealing her eggs. She bellows to warn the rest of the herd and many dinosaurs scatter in alarm. In the foreground, an early mammal perches on a branch near a magnolia—one of the earliest flowering plants.

LEAELLYNASAURA
aka LOOKOUT

A fast-running plant-eater, Leaellynasaura lived in a part of Australia that was inside the Antarctic Circle during the Cretaceous period.

BONUS FEATURE:
BIG EYES

This dinosaur had larger eyes than most dinosaurs of its size, so probably had extra-good eyesight.

VITAL STATISTICS

Order: Ornithischia
Family: Hypsilophodontidae
Period: Early Cretaceous
Home territory: Australia
Habitat: Cold regions
Size: 6–10 ft (2–3 m) long

DISTINGUISHING FEATURES

Leaellynasaura was a small, lightly built dinosaur, which moved upright on its long, slender back legs. Its large eyes helped it take advantage of any light there was during the long dark winters in its polar home.

COMBAT HISTORY

Leaellynasaura's main enemy was the ferocious dwarf allosaur that lived in the same area. Although smaller than other allosaurs, it was just as fierce and equipped with powerful jaws and sharp claws. Leaellynasaura's only hope was to run, and thanks to its speed and agility it did often manage to escape the hungry predator.

STRENGTH: 1
Too small and light to have much strength, Leaellynasaura was powerless against a fierce attacker.

ARMOR: 0
This dinosaur had no body armor and relied on escaping if danger threatened.

SPEED: 8
Like all hypsilophodonts, Leaellynasaura was a fast runner, able to reach top speed in seconds.

AGILITY: 8
With its light build, Leaellynasaura was supple and agile, able to leap and dart through the thickest forests as it searched for food or fled from enemies.

SCARINESS: 0
Leaellynasaura was a small plant-eater, so not a scary sight at all!

SPECIAL SKILLS: 5
There's safety in numbers when you're a plant-eater, so Leaellynasaura usually moved in herds. As the little dinosaurs fed on plants, they were always on the alert for danger. As soon as one was alarmed, the whole herd would take off.

KRONOSAURUS
aka FLIPPER

DANGER LEVEL 7.5

The tiger of the sea, this pliosaur was a ferocious underwater hunter and just as terrifying as the dinosaurs on land.

BONUS FEATURE:
THE BITE
Kronosaurus's huge jaws measured almost a quarter of its total length.

VITAL STATISTICS
Order: Plesiosauria
Family: Pliosauridae
Period: Early Cretaceous
Home territory: Australia
Habitat: Open ocean
Size: 42 ft (13 m) long

DISTINGUISHING FEATURES
Kronosaurus was the biggest of the marine reptiles known as pliosaurs. These fierce creatures had huge heads and jaws lined with strong, sharp teeth, so they could catch bigger prey than other marine reptiles. Its long flippers helped power it through the water.

COMBAT HISTORY
Kronosaurus would have had few enemies. Although some ichthyosaurs were larger, Kronosaurus, with its large jaws and sharp teeth, was fiercer and could win most battles.

STRENGTH: 9
This marine reptile was hugely strong, capable of overcoming most other sea creatures of the time.

ARMOR: 0
Kronosaurus had no body armor—but few creatures would have dared to attack this monster.

SPEED: 9
A fast swimmer, Kronosaurus moved with the help of its four powerful flippers.

AGILITY: 9
Kronosaurus was agile in the water, able to change direction with ease as it chased its prey. It could also drag itself along on land for short distances.

SCARINESS: 9
This mighty-jawed predator was one of the most terrifying sights in Cretaceous seas.

★ SPECIAL SKILLS: 9
Its strong teeth and jaws meant that Kronosaurus could prey on more or less anything it chose, including hard-shelled shellfish.

IGUANODON
aka THE JABBER

Plant-eating Iguanodon lived in herds, which roamed Cretaceous woodlands searching for food to eat. Iguanodon was only the second dinosaur to be discovered, back in the nineteenth century.

BONUS FEATURE:
THE THUMB
Iguanodon's thumb spike was a useful weapon for defending itself against attackers.

VITAL STATISTICS
Order: Ornithischia
Family: Iguanodontidae
Period: Early Cretaceous
Home territory: Europe, North America, Asia
Habitat: Woodlands
Size: 30 ft (9 m) long

DISTINGUISHING FEATURES
Iguanodon was a big, bulky animal with strong legs and hooflike nails on its feet. Its arms were shorter than its legs, but it generally walked on all fours. On each hand Iguanodon had a sharp spike instead of a thumb.

COMBAT HISTORY
If taken by surprise, Iguanodon was vulnerable to attack by packs of sharp-toothed hunters such as Deinonychus and Utahraptor. But with its great weight and strength it was often able to wound attackers and escape from their clutches.

STRENGTH: 8
With it large, muscular body, Iguanodon was a strong dinosaur, capable of defending itself from enemies.

ARMOR: 0
Iguanodon had no body armor—except its thumb spikes.

SPEED: 4
This dinosaur generally moved slowly as it wandered from plant to plant, but could run at up to 20 mph (30 km/h) if threatened.

AGILITY: 4
Although too bulky to be very agile, Iguanodon could rear up on two legs to feed on high plants.

SCARINESS: 6
A full-grown Iguanodon could weigh up to 7 tons, so was a daunting prospect for any predator.

SPECIAL SKILLS: 6
If attacked, Iguanodon could use its thumb spike to defend itself, driving it into its attacker's flesh or eyes.

Megalosaurus

Iguanodon herd

Hypsilophodon

⬆
A group of iguanodons feeding on the riverbank keeps a wary eye on an approaching Megalosaurus.

➡
Iguanodon could stand on two legs to reach high plants, using its strong tail as a prop to help hold itself up. Iguanodon had a powerful beak at the front of its jaws for chopping mouthfuls of tough plants. Farther back were strong teeth for chewing its food. New teeth grew as old ones wore out.

87

AMARGASAURUS
aka SPINY

DANGER LEVEL 6

This plant-eating dinosaur traveled in herds, feeding on conifer trees, ferns, and club mosses. The animals moved from place to place after eating all the plants in an area.

VITAL STATISTICS
Order: Saurischia
Family: Diplodocidae
Period: Early Cretaceous
Home territory: South America
Habitat: Open plains
Size: 33 ft (10 m) long

DISTINGUISHING FEATURES
Amargasaurus had two rows of spines along its backbone. These may have helped to protect it from predators. Or they may have been covered with skin, making a sail-like structure along the dinosaur's back.

STRENGTH: 7
Although smaller than others in its family, Amargasaurus was still a very large, powerful animal, weighing more than 3 tons (5,000 kg).

COMBAT HISTORY
Peaceful, plant-eating Amargasaurus would not have stood much chance if attacked by a fierce predator such as Carnotaurus. Such hunters wounded their prey with some vicious bites, then retreated until the animal slowly bled to death.

ARMOR: 3
The spines on Amargasaurus's back may have given it some protection, but it had no other armor.

SPEED: 4
Amargasaurus was not a fast mover and probably walked at about the same speed as we do—although it took much bigger steps!

AGILITY: 3
This dinosaur walked on all fours. It may have reared up on two legs to reach leaves high in the trees, using its tail to help balance and support its weight.

SCARINESS: 9
When alone, this dino wasn't all that fearsome, but a herd of them could take on all comers.

SPECIAL SKILLS: 10
Like most sauropods, Amargasaurus swallowed its plant food whole. It also swallowed stones to help grind down the food in its stomach.

SAUROPELTA
aka THE HULK

DANGER LEVEL 5.3

Built like a tank and covered with spikes and bony plates, Sauropelta was one of the largest of the armored dinosaurs.

VITAL STATISTICS
Order: Ornithischia
Family: Nodosauridae
Period: Early Cretaceous
Home territory: North America
Habitat: Woodland
Size: 25 ft (8 m) long

DISTINGUISHING FEATURES
This bulky creature had a long narrow head, a broad body, and short thick legs. The bony plates on its back were embedded in the skin, making a strong but flexible covering.

COMBAT HISTORY
Sauropelta was so well armored it was hard for any predator to attack—even mighty flesh-eaters such as Acrocanthosaurus. Provided it stood its ground and didn't allow an attacker to get at its more vulnerable underside, Sauropelta could beat most enemies.

STRENGTH: 7
With its heavy coat of armor, this massive dinosaur probably weighed as much as 3 tons and had a strong, muscular body.

ARMOR: 9
As well as the bony plates running from its neck to the end of its long tail, Sauropelta had spikes that stuck out from each side of its body. These made it very difficult for any predator to tackle.

SPEED: 2
Sauropelta was not a fast mover. If in danger, it would stay still and rely on its armor to keep it safe.

AGILITY: 1
Too bulky to run or jump, Sauropelta was not an agile dinosaur.

SCARINESS: 7
Only the bravest—or hungriest—hunters would dare attack this spiky giant.

SPECIAL SKILLS: 6
Like many plant-eaters, Sauropelta could gather its food with the toothless horny beak at the front of its jaws.

DEINONYCHUS vs. HYPSILOPHODON

THE BATTLE

TIME:
Early Cretaceous

PLACE:
North America: Montana

WINNER:
Deinonychus

Competitor ①

DEINONYCHUS

Order: Saurischia
Family: Dromaeosauridae
Size: 10–13 ft (3–4 m) long

Fast-moving hunter Deinonychus had special weapons for attacking its prey. On the second toe of each foot was a large curved claw that the dinosaur could use to slash at its victim.

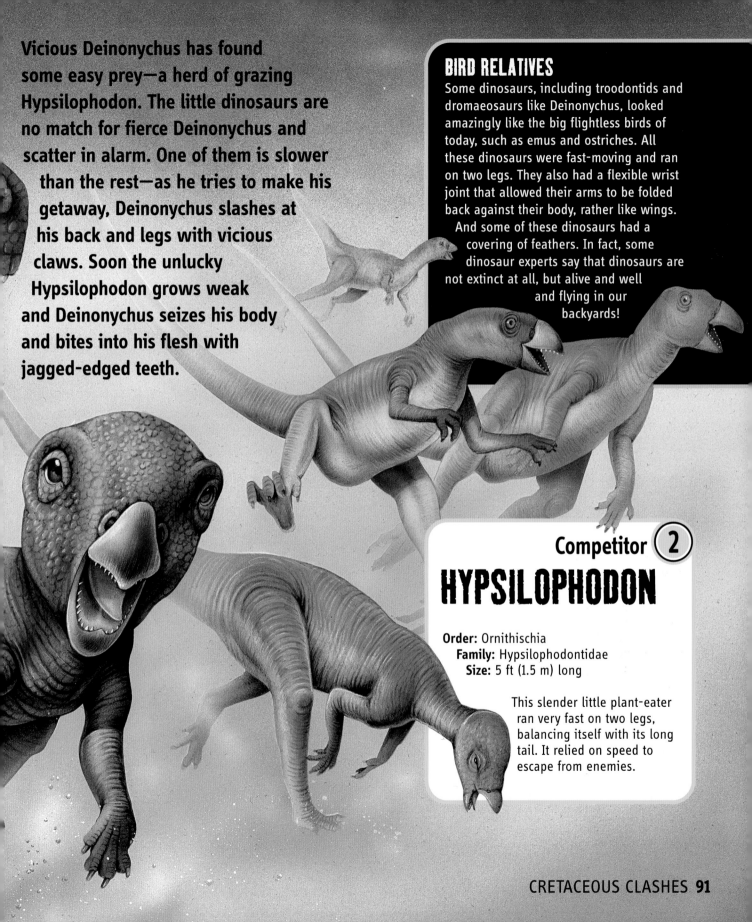

Vicious Deinonychus has found some easy prey—a herd of grazing Hypsilophodon. The little dinosaurs are no match for fierce Deinonychus and scatter in alarm. One of them is slower than the rest—as he tries to make his getaway, Deinonychus slashes at his back and legs with vicious claws. Soon the unlucky Hypsilophodon grows weak and Deinonychus seizes his body and bites into his flesh with jagged-edged teeth.

BIRD RELATIVES

Some dinosaurs, including troodontids and dromaeosaurs like Deinonychus, looked amazingly like the big flightless birds of today, such as emus and ostriches. All these dinosaurs were fast-moving and ran on two legs. They also had a flexible wrist joint that allowed their arms to be folded back against their body, rather like wings. And some of these dinosaurs had a covering of feathers. In fact, some dinosaur experts say that dinosaurs are not extinct at all, but alive and well and flying in our backyards!

Competitor (2)

HYPSILOPHODON

Order: Ornithischia
Family: Hypsilophodontidae
Size: 5 ft (1.5 m) long

This slender little plant-eater ran very fast on two legs, balancing itself with its long tail. It relied on speed to escape from enemies.

OURANOSAURUS
aka THE FIN

This large plant-eater was a member of the Iguanodon family. Like its relatives, Ouranosaurus had a sharp thumb spike on each hand, which it used to defend itself against unwary attackers.

VITAL STATISTICS
Order: Ornithischia
Family: Iguanodontidae
Period: Early Cretaceous
Home territory: Africa
Habitat: Open plains
Size: 23 ft (7 m) long

DISTINGUISHING FEATURES
Ouranosaurus had a row of spines running down its back. These were covered with skin, making a finlike structure. The fin may have helped the dinosaur control its temperature— it turned its fin into the sun to warm up and away to cool down.

COMBAT HISTORY
With its weight and strength, Ouranosaurus could best many predators. One of its enemies was a mighty meat-eater called Spinosaurus, which, like Ouranosaurus, had a large sail on its back. Spinosaurus was the larger animal so was likely to win any battles.

STRENGTH: 7
With its bulky body and heavy tail, Ouranosaurus weighed as much as 4 tons and was a powerful animal.

ARMOR: 4
Ouranosaurus had no body armor, but the large fin on its back would have made it more difficult for predators to attack.

SPEED: 2
Like all iguanodonts, Ouranosaurus was not a fast mover. It generally walked on all fours.

AGILITY: 3
Ouranosaurus was too heavy and big-boned to be agile, but it could rear up onto two legs to reach food or to run.

SCARINESS: 2
Few predators would have been afraid of Ouranosaurus. A peaceful plant-eater, it preferred to stay well away from trouble.

SPECIAL SKILLS: 6
Ouranosaurus's only weapon was its sharp thumb spike. Using this, Ouranosaurus could seriously wound or even blind an attacker.

WUERHOSAURUS
aka SURVIVOR

Chinese stegosaur Wuerhosaurus was one of the few in its family to survive into the Cretaceous period. Most stegosaurs died out toward the end of the Jurassic.

VITAL STATISTICS
Order: Ornithischia
Family: Stegosauridae
Period: Early Cretaceous
Home territory: Asia: China
Habitat: Woodland
Size: 20 ft (6 m) long

DISTINGUISHING FEATURES
Like all stegosaurs, Wuerhosaurus had a small head, huge body, and heavy tail. Along its back were rows of bony plates that were covered with blood-rich skin. These probably helped the dinosaur control its body temperature.

COMBAT HISTORY
Yangchuanosaurus was one of the largest meat-eating dinosaurs in the area at the time and, when hungry enough, would tackle even this spiky stegosaur. If it could avoid Wuerhosaurus's lashing tail and get near enough to attack the plant-eater's unprotected belly, the predator could hope for a victory over the stegosaur.

STRENGTH: 8
With its huge, bulky body and pillarlike legs, Wuerhosaurus was an extremely powerful animal.

ARMOR: 1
Although the bony plates on its back were probably evolved as a form of temperature control, they also made Wuerhosaurus more difficult to attack. It could also use the bony spikes on its tail to defend itself against an enemy.

SPEED: 2
Stegosaurs were not fast runners. When attacked they probably stood their ground and relied on their armor.

AGILITY: 3
Wuerhosaurus could not rear up and run on two legs but may have been able to stand up on its back legs for a few moments to feed on high plants.

SCARINESS: 6
With their back plates, tail spikes, and sheer bulk, all stegosaurs were scary-looking creatures.

SPECIAL SKILLS: 7
If in danger, Wuerhosaurus could lash its spiked tail back and forth to wound an attacker.

CARNOTAURUS

aka THE BULL

This dinosaur's name means "meat-eating bull," and its horns certainly give it a bull-like appearance. Carnotaurus was one of the largest, fiercest hunters in Cretaceous South America.

VITAL STATISTICS

Order: Saurischia
Family: Abelisauridae
Period: Mid to Late Cretaceous
Home territory: South America: Argentina
Habitat: Plains
Size: 24 ft 6 in (7.5 m) long

DISTINGUISHING FEATURES

Carnotaurus had a big bull-like head topped with a pair of sharp horns. Its body and back legs were strong and muscular, but its arms were extremely small and almost useless.

COMBAT HISTORY

This dinosaur's arms were too small for grabbing prey so it had to seize its victims with its teeth while slashing at them with a clawed foot. Plant-eaters such as duckbills and iguanodonts would have steered well clear of this horned monster.

STRENGTH: 7

This massive hunter weighed as much as a ton and had a powerful, muscular body. But despite the size of its head, its jaws were surprisingly weak.

ARMOR: 7

Carnotaurus's body was covered with small cone-shaped spines, which would have helped protect it from the claws of struggling prey.

SPEED: 8

Like most meat-eating dinosaurs, Carnotaurus could run at high speed as it chased prey across the South American plains.

AGILITY: 7

Long back legs made this large creature surprisingly agile, able to jump with ease as it ambushed prey.

SCARINESS: 8

Not held back by its tiny arms, Carnotaurus was an awe-inspiring predator and would have terrified most sensible creatures of the time.

SPECIAL SKILLS: 8

Carnotaurus could have used its tough horns in head-butting contests with rivals as well as for attacking prey.

PENTACERATOPS
aka FIVE HORNS

DANGER LEVEL **5.7**

Liked other horned dinosaurs, Pentaceratops lived in peaceful herds that moved through the Cretaceous forests, chopping off mouthfuls of tough plants with their strong beaks.

VITAL STATISTICS
Order: Ornithischia
Family: Ceratopsidae
Period: Late Cretaceous
Home territory: North America
Habitat: Forests
Size: 20 ft (6 m) long

DISTINGUISHING FEATURES
This horned dinosaur had a huge bony neck frill, fringed with lots of small spines, as well as five sharp horns on its massive head. It had a bulky body and sturdy pillarlike legs.

COMBAT HISTORY
Tyrannosaurus would track a herd of horned dinosaurs, watching for one that seemed slower or more vulnerable than the others. It then crept up on its victim, approaching from behind if possible, and wounding the horned dinosaur's unprotected flanks. With luck, Pentaceratops could see off its attacker with a lunge of its mighty horned head.

STRENGTH: 7
A hugely powerful animal, Pentaceratops had the strength to withstand the attacks of most other animals.

ARMOR: 9
Pentaceratops was extremely well armored. Its bony neck frill protected its neck and shoulders, often the most vulnerable areas of a dinosaur.

SPEED: 2
Weighed down by its bulky armor, Pentaceratops was a slow mover and tended to stand its ground rather than try to flee from attack.

AGILITY: 1
There was no way that a horned dinosaur such as Pentaceratops could jump or rear up on two legs.

SCARINESS: 8
Just the sight of this creature would have been enough to frighten off all but the most determined enemies.

SPECIAL SKILLS: 7
If necessary, Pentaceratops could defend itself with its sharp horns, even charging its enemy like a giant rhinoceros.

EUOPLOCEPHALUS
aka THE CLUBBER

DANGER LEVEL 6

Euoplocephalus belonged to the ankylosaur, or armored dinosaur, group. These sturdy creatures traveled in herds, fed on plants, and depended on their strength and body armor to protect them from enemies.

BONUS FEATURE:
TAIL CLUB
This dinosaur had a heavy bony club at the end of its tail that could deal any attacker a deadly blow.

VITAL STATISTICS
Order: Ornithischia
Family: Ankylosauridae
Period: Late Cretaceous
Home territory: North America
Habitat: Open plains
Size: 18 ft (5.5 m) long

DISTINGUISHING FEATURES
Ankylosaurs like Euoplocephalus were so heavily armored that even their eyelids were protected. Pieces of bone came down like shutters over the normal lids to protect the dinosaur's eyes from sharp claws.

COMBAT HISTORY
If threatened, Euoplocephalus could become a terrifying opponent as it lashed its clubbed tail to and fro. A predator's best hope was to try to attack its unprotected underside.

STRENGTH: 8
This sturdy creature had particularly strong hip and back muscles, which helped it swing its huge tail club from side to side to defend itself.

ARMOR: 9
Amazingly well armored, Euoplocephalus's heavy body was covered with plates of bone set into its leather skin. Its back was also studded with lots of sharp spikes.

SPEED: 2
This dinosaur was not a fast mover, but it had no need to be—with armor like this it could stand its ground against most attackers.

AGILITY: 1
Euoplocephalus moved on all fours—its leg bones were extra sturdy to support the weight of its armor—and could not rear up on two legs.

SCARINESS: 8
Euoplocephalus was scary enough on its own, but a herd of these club-tailed dinosaurs was more than most predators wanted to take on.

SPECIAL SKILLS: 8
The club at the end of Euoplocephalus's tail weighed about 60 lb (27 kg). A blow from this bony weapon could smash the leg of even a large predator such as Tyrannosaurus.

DROMAEOSAURUS
aka THE CLAW

Dromaeosaurus wasn't one of the largest dinosaurs, but it was certainly one of the most vicious. These fast-moving predators hunted in packs and could bring down creatures much larger than themselves.

BONUS FEATURE:
SHARP TALON
On each foot Dromaeosaurus had an extra-large, sickle-shaped claw, which it used like a dagger to slash through a victim's flesh.

VITAL STATISTICS
Order: Saurischia
Family: Dromaeosauridae
Period: Late Cretaceous
Home territory: North America
Habitat: Woodland and plains
Size: 6 ft (1.8 m)

DISTINGUISHING FEATURES
Dromaeosaurus had a lightly built body, long tail, and long slender back legs. It had large eyes and long narrow jaws packed with sharp teeth.

COMBAT HISTORY
A pack of Dromaeosaurus hunting together could bring down much larger creatures, including duckbill dinosaurs such as Saurolophus. Dromaeosaurs were merciless as they surrounded their victim, some clawing at its legs, others leaping on its back.

STRENGTH: 5
This dinosaur relied on speed and cunning more than brute force, but it had strong hands and feet, which it used to grip and slash at its prey.

ARMOR: 0
Dromaeosaurus had no body armor—but it didn't reckon on staying still long enough to need any.

SPEED: 9
This dinosaur was built for speed and may have raced along at up to 30 mph (50 km/h). When running it held its large sickle claws up off the ground so they didn't get blunt.

AGILITY: 9
Muscular and supple, Dromaeosaurus was amazingly agile and could leap up off the ground to attack its victims.

SCARINESS: 8
For a small dinosaur, Dromaeosaurus was very scary. It was so terrifying, in fact, that most other creatures of the time would want to stay well away from it!

SPECIAL SKILLS: 8
Dromaeosaurus could stand on one foot with ease as it slashed its victim's skin with its other clawed foot. These large, curved foot claws were as much as 5 in (13 cm) long.

BATTLE TACTIC: ARMOR

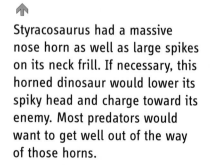

Some dinosaurs relied on speed to protect them from danger. Others, such as many of the sauropods, were just too big for most predators. For others, body armor was the best defense. If attacked, armored dinosaurs could just stand still while the predator tried to find a way through the spikes and studs—and very often gave up.

Some of the most heavily armored dinosaurs were ankylosaurs and nodosaurs. Typically, the necks, backs, sides, and tails of these dinosaurs were covered with large flat plates of bone set into the thick skin. Spikes and bony knobs also studded their bodies.

Horned dinosaurs boasted huge frills of bone at the back of the neck and sharp horns on their heads. Stegosaurs had yet another kind of body armor. These massive dinosaurs had double rows of bony plates on their backs. No one is sure what these were for, but many experts think that they helped the dinosaurs control their body temperature. They would also have helped protect the stegosaur from predators.

Styracosaurus had a massive nose horn as well as large spikes on its neck frill. If necessary, this horned dinosaur would lower its spiky head and charge toward its enemy. Most predators would want to get well out of the way of those horns.

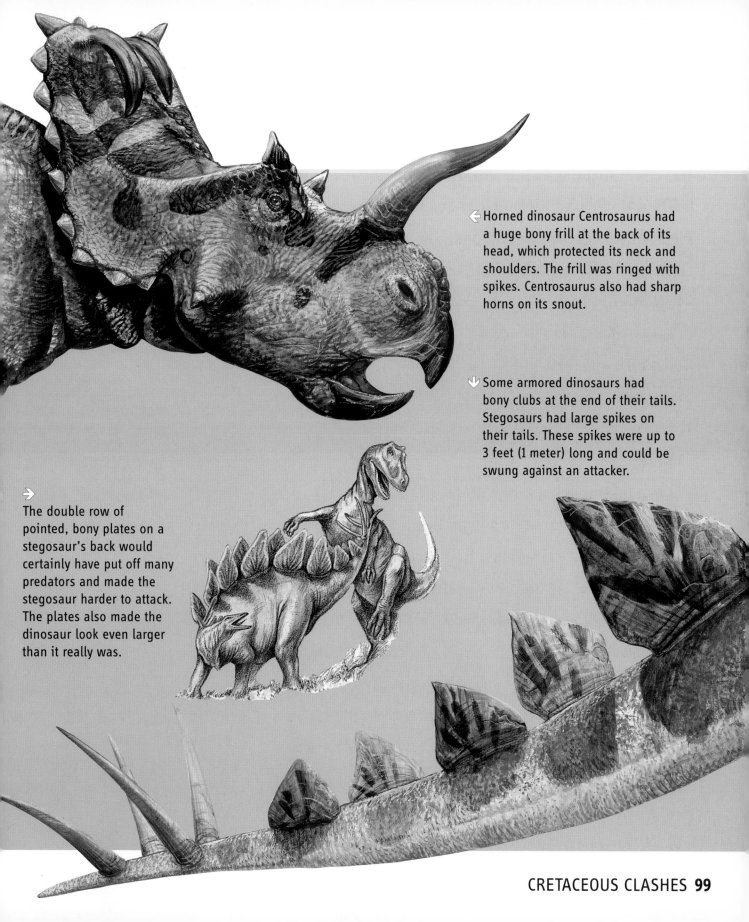

← Horned dinosaur Centrosaurus had a huge bony frill at the back of its head, which protected its neck and shoulders. The frill was ringed with spikes. Centrosaurus also had sharp horns on its snout.

⬇ Some armored dinosaurs had bony clubs at the end of their tails. Stegosaurs had large spikes on their tails. These spikes were up to 3 feet (1 meter) long and could be swung against an attacker.

→ The double row of pointed, bony plates on a stegosaur's back would certainly have put off many predators and made the stegosaur harder to attack. The plates also made the dinosaur look even larger than it really was.

ARCHELON

aka THE GIANT

DANGER LEVEL 3.2

This giant turtle was the size of a car. It moved slowly through shallow waters, feeding on fish and jellyfish as well as water plants. Like turtles today, it came to land once a year to lay its eggs.

VITAL STATISTICS
Order: Testudines
Family: Protostegidae
Period: Late Cretaceous
Home territory: North America
Habitat: The ocean
Size: 15 ft (4.5 m) long

DISTINGUISHING FEATURES
Archelon didn't have a heavy shell like most turtles. Instead its body was protected by a framework of bony struts covered with a thick layer of rubbery skin.

COMBAT HISTORY
Few other sea creatures would want to attack anything this size, so Archelon didn't have many enemies. However, if a hungry pliosaur or ichthyosaur did try to attack, Archelon had few defenses.

STRENGTH: 2
Despite its size, Archelon had weak jaws and no real weapons with which to defend itself.

ARMOR: 4
Archelon's leathery shell gave it some protection but, unlike most turtles and tortoises, it couldn't pull its head inside its shell, making it vulnerable to attack.

SPEED: 2
Archelon propelled itself through the water with its long flippers, but was not a fast mover.

AGILITY: 2
Like all turtles, Archelon was most at home in the water, but could drag itself along on land for short distances.

SCARINESS: 4
A turtle this size must have been an awe-inspiring sight, but Archelon was a gentle creature that preferred to stay well away from trouble.

SPECIAL SKILLS: 5
Archelon had a sharp beak at the front of its jaws for snapping up plants and cracking open shellfish.

DEINOSUCHUS
aka THE CHAMP

Deinosuchus means "terrible crocodile"—a good name for this monster. It was the biggest crocodile of all time and more than twice the length of the largest crocodiles today.

VITAL STATISTICS
Order: Crocodylia
Family: Alligatoridae
Period: Late Cretaceous
Home territory: North America
Habitat: Rivers and land
Size: 49 ft (15 m) long

DISTINGUISHING FEATURES
Like crocodiles now, Deinosuchus had a long body that was studded with bony plates, short legs, and a long tail. Its mighty jaws could open very wide and were lined with more than 100 large, sharp teeth.

COMBAT HISTORY
This huge crocodile was a top predator, ready to attack almost anything that came its way—even giant meat-eating dinosaurs such as Tyrannosaurus!

STRENGTH: 9
This giant was immensely strong, capable of attacking prey as large, if not larger than, itself.

ARMOR: 8
Deinosuchus's body was protected by bony plates set into tough skin.

SPEED: 8
An expert swimmer, Deinosuchus was capable of moving through the water with scarcely a sound and sweeping up on prey.

AGILITY: 7
Deinosuchus could also move fairly fast on land and would come out of the water to chase prey if it had to.

SCARINESS: 9
A small crocodile is scary enough, so one this size would have terrified most other animals of the time.

SPECIAL SKILLS: 9
Deinosuchus was skilled at ambushing prey. The crocodile lay in the water, only its eyes above the surface, watching for animals coming to the riverbank to drink. Deinosuchus then lunged toward its victim, dragging it into the water while tearing it apart with its strong teeth.

GALLIMIMUS VS. TARBOSAURUS

THE BATTLE

TIME:
Late Cretaceous

PLACE:
Asia

WINNER:
Tarbosaurus

Inch by inch, a huge Tarbosaurus has crept toward a group of Gallimimus dinosaurs as they feed. As soon as one Gallimimus gets a whiff of the big predator's scent, the group takes off at top speed with Tarbosaurus panting along behind. The tyrannosaur can't keep up with these fast runners for long, but one younger, weaker animal has fallen slightly behind—and that is his downfall.

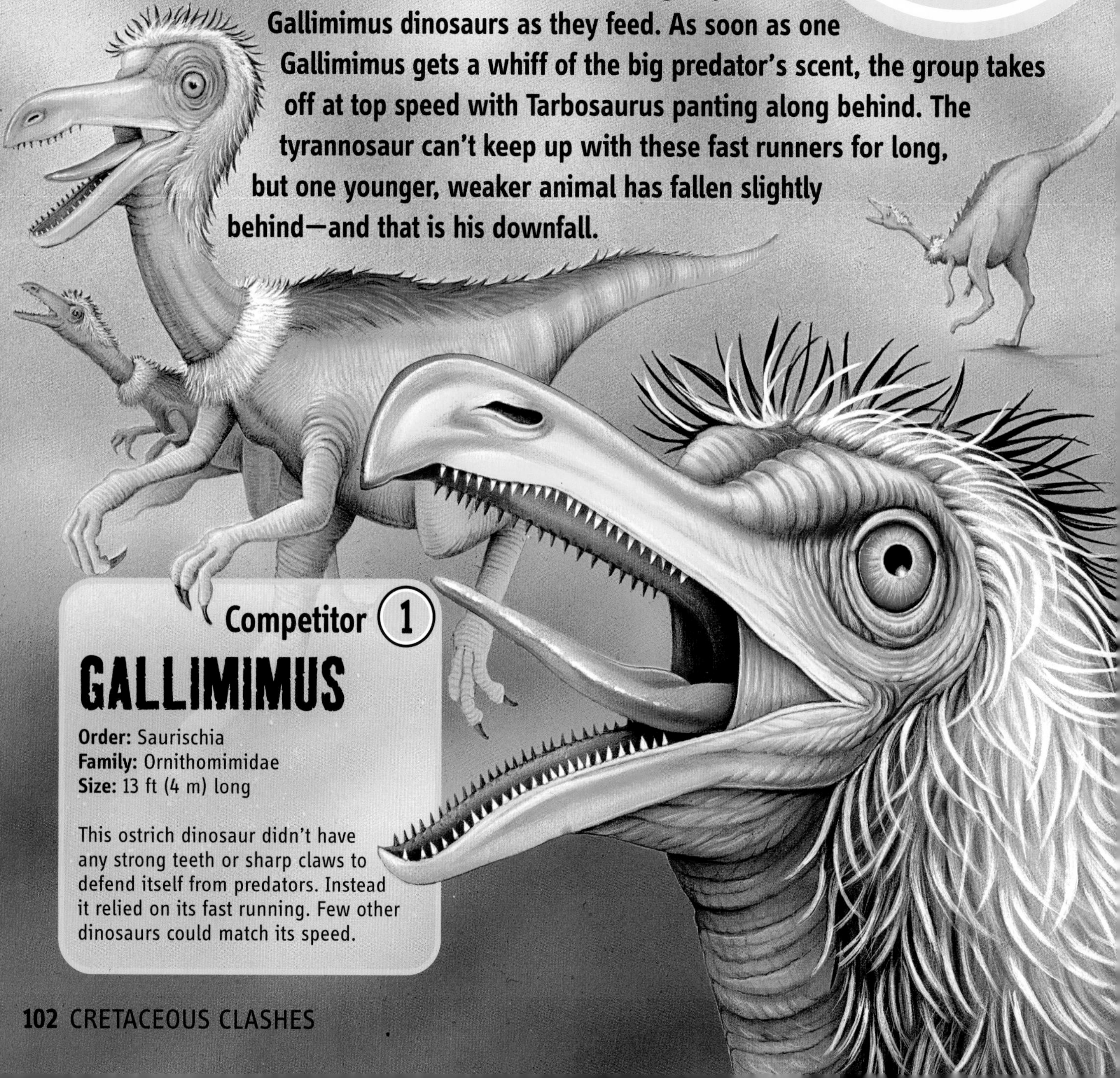

Competitor 1

GALLIMIMUS

Order: Saurischia
Family: Ornithomimidae
Size: 13 ft (4 m) long

This ostrich dinosaur didn't have any strong teeth or sharp claws to defend itself from predators. Instead it relied on its fast running. Few other dinosaurs could match its speed.

TARBOSAURUS

Order: Saurischia
Family: Tyrannosauridae
Size: 46 ft (14 m) long

Like all tyrannosaurs, this huge meat-eater had a massive head and strong jaws lined with sharp teeth. Its back legs were big and bulky, but its arms were so small, they were almost useless.

PROTOCERATOPS

aka BEAKY

DANGER LEVEL **4.5**

Herds of Protoceratops dinosaurs roamed the vast plains of what is now Mongolia in Asia. Hundreds of skeletons of this dinosaur have been found, ranging from tiny babies to adult males and females.

BONUS FEATURE:
STRONG BEAK

The powerful toothless beak at the front of this dinosaur's jaws helped it chomp down plenty of tough plants, such as cycads.

VITAL STATISTICS

Order: Ornithischia
Family: Protoceratopidae
Period: Late Cretaceous
Home territory: Asia: Mongolia
Habitat: Scrubland
Size: 9 ft (2.7 m)

DISTINGUISHING FEATURES

One of the smaller horned dinosaurs, Protoceratops had a large head with a bony neck frill. Males had bigger neck frills than females.

COMBAT HISTORY

Protoceratops had to keep a lookout for large tyrannosaurs such as Alioramus, which could easily overcome its defenses. Packs of smaller hunters such as Velociraptor would also attack Protoceratops and sometimes manage to win the battle.

STRENGTH: 6

With its bulky body and sturdy legs, Protoceratops was strong enough to fight back when attacked.

ARMOR: 6

Protoceratops's bony neck frill provided some defense from attackers, and a large bump on its snout protected its head in battles with enemies or rivals.

SPEED: 2

This dinosaur was slow-moving and tended to stand its ground and rely on its bulk if threatened, rather than running for cover.

AGILITY: 5

Although not able to jump and rear up on two legs, Protoceratops was surprisingly nimble and could turn quickly to nip an enemy with its powerful beaked jaws.

SCARINESS: 3

Protoceratops was not one of the scariest horned dinosaurs, but its massive head and heavy beak still made it an impressive sight.

SPECIAL SKILLS: 5

There's strength in numbers and, together, a herd of Protoceratops stood a chance of fending off an attacker.

CHASMOSAURUS
aka FRILLS

DANGER LEVEL 6

Despite its fearsome appearance, Chasmosaurus was a plant-eating dinosaur that meant no harm to anyone. But if threatened, it would use its huge neck frill and horns to warn off its enemies.

BONUS FEATURE:
SHARP HORNS

A pair of curving horns on the top of its head and a shorter horn on its snout helped Chasmosaurus protect itself.

VITAL STATISTICS
Order: Ornithischia
Family: Ceratopsidae
Period: Late Cretaceous
Home territory: North America
Habitat: Forests
Size: 17 ft (5 m)

DISTINGUISHING FEATURES
This dinosaur had a huge bony neck frill stretching from the back of its head and covering its neck and shoulders. The frill was studded with lots of bony knobs and spikes.

COMBAT HISTORY
If threatened, Chasmosaurus would lower its huge horned head and try to charge the attacker. A giant predator, such as Tyrannosaurus, could probably overcome the horned dinosaur after a struggle, but would have preferred easier prey.

STRENGTH: 7
Chasmosaurus had to be strong to carry just its body armor around. Its body was bulky and powerful and its legs muscular and pillarlike to support its weight.

ARMOR: 7
The bony neck frill provided plenty of protection for this dinosaur's vulnerable head and neck area and made it hard for other dinosaurs to attack.

SPEED: 3
This dinosaur was not a fast mover and relied on strength and bulk for defense, not speed. Its feet are the feet of a plodder, not a fast runner.

AGILITY: 5
Chasmosaurus was not able to rear up on two legs, but could turn quickly to charge an attacker.

SCARINESS: 7
Its bony armor made this dinosaur a threatening sight and gave it the appearance of being bigger than it really was.

SPECIAL SKILLS: 7
Chasmosaurus lived in herds. Palaeontologists believe that, if the group was in danger, the dinosaurs would stand in a ring with the young at the center, and, like the modern musk oxen, shake their massive heads to warn off enemies.

QUETZALCOATLUS
aka JUMBO

DANGER LEVEL
6

The biggest flying creature that has ever lived, Quetzalcoatlus was also one of the last pterosaurs to evolve. This giant lived right up to the end of the Cretaceous.

VITAL STATISTICS
Order: Pterosauria
Family: Azhdarchidae
Period: Late Cretaceous
Home territory: North America
Habitat: Marshland
Size: 39 ft (12 m) from wingtip to wingtip

DISTINGUISHING FEATURES
This huge pterosaur had vast wings, but its body was small and lightly built. It had a long neck and long, slender, toothless jaws.

COMBAT HISTORY
Quetzalcoatlus was really only at risk from predators when on land. If attacked by a large meat-eating dinosaur, or a crocodile such as Deinosuchus, Quetzalcoatlus would fight back with its sharp beak and beating wings. But it didn't have the strength to resist for long and its light fragile bones were easily broken by a predator's powerful jaws.

STRENGTH: 7
A pterosaur this size needed very powerful muscles to beat its mighty wings.

ARMOR: 0
Quetzalcoatlus had no body armor. In the air it had no enemies, but on the ground it was vulnerable to attack.

SPEED: 8
Quetzalcoatlus was a fast flier and an expert glider, able to soar for miles with scarcely a beat of its wings.

AGILITY: 7
Like most pterosaurs, Quetzalcoatlus was very agile in the air and could swoop down to grab prey from land or sea.

SCARINESS: 7
Size alone made this pterosaur an awe-inspiring sight, but it had no sharp teeth or claws to defend itself from enemies.

SPECIAL SKILLS: 7
As well as scooping up prey from the sea or marshland, Quetzalcoatlus may have used its long, slender jaws to tear flesh from the bodies of dead animals, rather like vultures today.

GIGANOTOSAURUS
aka HUNTER

One of the largest of all meat-eating animals ever to have lived on Earth, Giganotosaurus weighed a massive 8 tons. Imagine a fierce, sharp-toothed hunter that was even bigger than an elephant, and you'll get the idea!

VITAL STATISTICS
Order: Saurischia
Family: Abelisauridae
Period: Late Cretaceous
Home territory: South America
Habitat: Open plains
Size: 43 ft (14 m) long

DISTINGUISHING FEATURES
Giganotosaurus had a massive head: at 6 feet (2 meters) long, it was as long as a human! The huge jaws were lined with teeth the size of steak knives.

COMBAT HISTORY
Giganotosaurus could crush more or less anything in its mighty jaws. Even sauropods—giant plant-eating dinosaurs such as Saltasaurus—weren't safe from this hunter.

STRENGTH: 10
This powerfully built creature was immensely strong, able to tear almost any other animal to pieces in seconds.

ARMOR: 4
Gigantosaurus had no body armor, but who was going to attack an animal with a mouth full of 8-inch (20-cm) teeth?

SPEED: 8
Like other carnosaurs, Giganotosaurus walked upright on its massive back legs. It could probably run fast for a brief time when chasing prey.

AGILITY: 8
Despite its bulk, Giganotosaurus was able to leap and pounce as it attacked its victims.

SCARINESS: 10
Giganotosaurus was certainly one of the most terrifying creatures that has ever lived.

SPECIAL SKILLS: 10
As well as hunting its own prey, this monster stole prey from other predators. One look from this bully and smaller hunters would give up their meal.

BATTLE TACTIC: SCARINESS

What's scarier than a mouth full of razor-sharp teeth and claws that tear and rip? Like animals today, dinosaurs spent much of their time finding enough food to eat. Hunters had to track down and catch their prey, but one good meal could last them for days. The largest meat-eaters, such as tyrannosaurs, were so ferocious, they could attack even the biggest plant-eaters. Part of the strategy of large hunters such as Allosaurus and Tarbosaurus was surprise. The hunter would lie in wait until the prey came near, then leap out, sinking its teeth into the victim's flesh and slashing its hide with sharp claws. But the huge plant-eaters were not easily intimidated and would fight to the bitter end. The predator's best tactic was to wound its victim as severely as possible and then stay well clear until it became too weak to move.

Smaller predators, such as Velociraptor and Dromaeosaurus, were scary too, because they hunted in packs. Together they could bring down prey much larger than themselves. These vicious creatures would fling themselves onto a large plant-eater and bite and claw while trying to keep out of the way of huge limbs and sharp horns.

⬆
Deinonychus wasn't one of the largest dinosaurs, but it was a terrifying hunter. It had a large head and powerful jaws lined with curved teeth. These teeth had serrated edges like a steak knife and could cut through flesh with ease.

➡
Fierce hunter Dromaeosaurus had a lethal weapon on each foot—a huge, curved claw which was up to 5 inches (13 cm) long. When attacking its victim, the dinosaur stood on one leg, while kicking with the other and slashing through the prey's flesh with the daggerlike claw.

Tarbosaurus

Gallimimus

A Gallimimus flees in panic, but threatening Tarbosaurus is hot on its heels. Gallimimus doesn't stand a chance once the predator is near enough to seize the smaller dinosaur in its mighty jaws.

VELOCIRAPTOR
aka THE RUNNER

DANGER LEVEL **6.5**

This ferocious little dinosaur's name means "speedy thief." It probably ate anything it could catch and often hunted in packs. Velociraptor certainly proved the rule that there's strength in numbers!

BONUS FEATURE:
THE LEGS
Velociraptor's slender back legs and narrow feet were ideal for fast running when hunting down its prey.

VITAL STATISTICS
Order: Saurischia
Family: Dromaeosauridae
Period: Late Cretaceous
Home territory: Asia
Habitat: Desert
Size: 6 ft (1.8 m) long

DISTINGUISHING FEATURES
Velociraptor was a lightly built dinosaur with long jaws and plenty of razor-sharp teeth. It may have had a feathery coat covering much of its body. On each foot it had an extra-large claw for attacking prey.

COMBAT HISTORY
Alone, Velociraptor hunted small or young plant-eating dinosaurs. In a pack these hunters could tackle creatures much larger than themselves, working together to wound their prey with their foot talons and sharp-clawed hands. If attacked, Velociraptor fought back viciously.

STRENGTH: 5
This dinosaur was speedy rather than strong, but it was powerful enough to attack and kill prey.

ARMOR: 0
Velociraptor had no body armor so needed to keep well away from enemies.

SPEED: 9
This long-legged hunter could race along at up to 30 mph (50 km/h) and overtake many other dinosaurs.

AGILITY: 9
Velociraptor was a very agile creature, able to leap up onto a larger animal's back to attack.

SCARINESS: 8
Velociraptors were small but often hunted in packs. Together, they were deadly opponents.

SPECIAL SKILLS: 8
Fossils of Velociraptor's skull show that it had a large brain and so was probably more intelligent than many dinosaurs. It probably had good eyesight and excellent hearing—vital for a hunter.

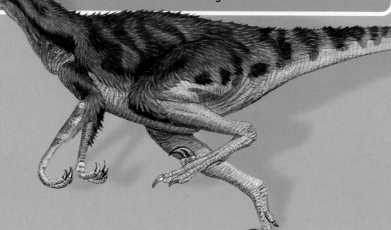

SUCHOMIMUS
aka THE THUMB

DANGER LEVEL **7.8**

One of the largest predators in Cretaceous Africa, this deadly creature was almost as big as Tyrannosaurus. As if that weren't enough, it also had long jaws like a giant, toothy crocodile.

BONUS FEATURE:
THE CLAWS
Suchomimus had massive claws, measuring as much as 16 inches (40 cm). Few animals stood a chance against these weapons.

VITAL STATISTICS
Order: Saurischia
Family: Spinosauridae
Period: Early Cretaceous
Home territory: Africa
Habitat: Plains
Size: 33 ft (10 m) long

DISTINGUISHING FEATURES
Suchomimus's long jaws were lined with more than 100 sharp teeth. On its back were spikes that may have supported a sail-like structure, probably used for controlling its body temperature.

COMBAT HISTORY
This huge predator could have attacked even big plant-eaters such as duckbill dinosaurs and sauropods. With its enormous claws, it could easily wound a much larger animal.

STRENGTH: 9
Hugely strong, this dinosaur was capable of ripping prey apart with its powerful clawed hands and sharp-toothed jaws.

ARMOR: 5
Suchomimus had no body armor but the spikes or sail on its back would have made it an even more fearsome prospect.

SPEED: 8
This dinosaur walked upright on its strong back legs and could probably run fast as it chased prey.

AGILITY: 7
Suchomimus could run and jump with ease and use its small, but strong, front legs to seize and hold its victims.

SCARINESS: 9
This was a truly terrifying creature, able to destroy more or less anything it came across.

SPECIAL SKILLS: 9
Suchomimus may have been able to catch fish as well as larger prey in the rivers and oceans, trapping them in its long, crocodile-like jaws.

DROMICEIOMIMUS
aka LEGGY

DANGER LEVEL **5.8**

Long-legged Dromiceiomimus was a fast-running dinosaur that fed on small creatures such as lizards. It was also able to dig for the eggs of other reptiles using its long arms.

VITAL STATISTICS
Order: Saurischia
Family: Ornithomimidae
Period: Late Cretaceous
Home territory: North America
Habitat: Varied
Size: 11 ft 6 in (3.5 m) long

DISTINGUISHING FEATURES
Dromiceiomimus was about the size of an ostrich today. As well as long, powerful hind legs, it had fairly long arms that it used to catch small animals and dig for eggs. Its head was small and it had narrow beaklike jaws.

COMBAT HISTORY
Dromiceiomimus would have needed its speed to escape from some of the mighty predators that lived alongside it—huge meat-eaters such as Albertosaurus.

STRENGTH: 5
Dromiceiomimus had strong leg and thigh muscles to power its fast running.

ARMOR: 0
This dinosaur had no protective body armor so relied on getting away from its enemies—fast.

SPEED: 9
Dromiceiomimus ran upright on its back legs and could reach speeds of up to 40 mph (65 km/h).

AGILITY: 9
Light and nimble, Dromiceiomimus could leap to snap up fast-moving insects from the air.

SCARINESS: 4
With its small head and weak jaws, Dromiceiomimus was not a frightening creature, but was perfectly adapted for its particular lifestyle.

SPECIAL SKILLS: 8
Dromiceiomimus had large eyes and probably very good eyesight, so it would have been able to search for food at dusk when light was poor. This dinosaur also had a large brain and so was probably very quick-witted.

PARASAUROLOPHUS
aka THE ECHO

Parasaurolophus belonged to the duckbilled dinosaur group. These were plant-eating dinosaurs with long back legs and shorter front legs. Duckbills traveled in herds, and get their name from the long, flattened beak at the front of their jaws.

VITAL STATISTICS
Order: Ornithischia
Family: Hadrosauridae
Period: Late Cretaceous
Home territory: North America
Habitat: Woodland and swamps
Size: 30 ft (9 m) long

DISTINGUISHING FEATURES
Parasaurolophus's head was topped with a large, backward-pointing crest, which was nearly 6 feet 6 inches (2 meters) long. The crest may have fitted into a notch in the dinosaur's backbone when its head was held up.

COMBAT HISTORY
Duckbilled dinosaurs such as Parasaurolophus were common prey for large meat-eaters such as the deadly Albertosaurus and Tyrannosaurus.

STRENGTH: 8
Parasaurolophus was a large, strong animal, but had no special weapons for defending itself from enemies.

ARMOR: 0
Although this dinosaur was heavily built, it had no body armor to protect itself from attack.

SPEED: 7
Like other duckbilled dinosaurs, Parasaurolophus spent much of its time on all fours, feeding on plants, but could rear up on its back legs to sprint away from predators.

AGILITY: 7
Parasaurolophus had a long, flexible neck, which allowed it to reach plants from a wide area around it, without having to move too often.

SCARINESS: 2
Apart from its loud call, Parasaurolophus had no way of scaring other animals.

SPECIAL SKILLS: 6
This dinosaur's crest was hollow and may have acted as an echo chamber to make its booming calls even louder. If one animal sounded the alarm, the others were quick to flee.

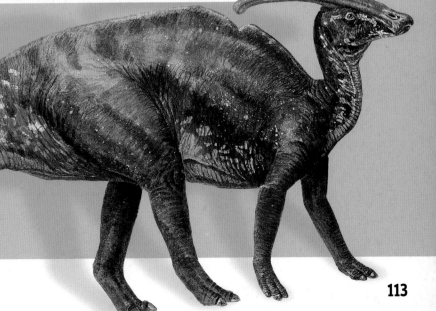

113

MOSASAURUS HOFFMANI
aka THE WHOPPER

DANGER LEVEL **7.1**

Mosasaurs were giant marine lizards that lived in all the world's oceans during the Late Cretaceous. Mosasaurus hoffmani was the largest of the group.

BONUS FEATURE:
POWERFUL TAIL
Mosasaurus used its huge tail to push itself through the water at high speed.

VITAL STATISTICS
Order: Squamata
Family: Mosasauridae
Period: Late Cretaceous
Home territory: Europe, North America, Africa, Australia, New Zealand
Habitat: The oceans
Size: 50 ft (15 m) long

DISTINGUISHING FEATURES
Mosasaurus had a long, streamlined body and four short paddle-like flippers. Its enormous jaws were up to 4 feet, 6 inches (1.4 meters) long and filled with sharp, curved teeth.

COMBAT HISTORY
Mosasaurus could snap up fish and ammonites with ease, but it was large and strong enough also to attack other marine reptiles such as plesiosaurs. A top predator in Cretaceous seas, Mosasaurus could win most of its battles.

STRENGTH: 8
This giant reptile was a powerful animal with a very strong tail.

ARMOR: 0
Mosasaurus had no body armor, but an animal of this size didn't really need protection.

SPEED: 8
Like other mosasaurs, Mosasaurus hoffmani was a fast swimmer able to power through the water at high speed as it pursued its prey.

AGILITY: 8
This reptile was agile, too, and steered with movements of its paddle-like legs.

SCARINESS: 10
With its vast jaws open wide, Mosasaurus would have been one of the most awe-inspiring sights in Cretaceous seas. And this monster would have been able to snap up almost anything that came its way.

SPECIAL SKILLS: 9
Each of this mosasaur's cone-shaped teeth had lots of cutting edges, enabling it to chomp down on more or less any other creature in the sea.

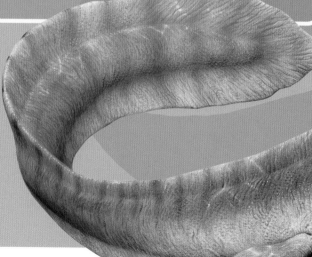

AN AMAZING FIND

Huge jawbones belonging to Mosasaurus hoffmani were found in a quarry near Maastricht in Holland in 1770. When the bones were first discovered, some experts thought they belonged to a whale. It was not until years later that scientists realized that these were the jawbones of a mosasaur—a giant sea-dwelling lizard that lived in the days of the dinosaurs. At that time water would have covered the area that is now Holland and lots of sea creatures would have lived there. The engraving above shows the discovery of the massive jawbones.

THERIZINOSAURUS
aka FINGERS

This extraordinary dinosaur had three huge claws, measuring 27 inches (70 cm) long, on each hand. Experts are still finding out about this dinosaur, but some think that Therizinosaurus may have used its long claws to gather plants and stuff them into its mouth.

VITAL STATISTICS
Order: Saurischia
Family: Therizinosauridae
Period: Late Cretaceous
Home territory: Asia
Habitat: Open plains
Size: 13–16 ft (4–5 m) long

DISTINGUISHING FEATURES
Therizinosaurus had a long neck and a small head. Its body may have been covered with a coat of feathers.

COMBAT HISTORY
Despite its big claws, Therizinosaurus could not put up much of a fight against predators such as Alioramus and deadly Tarbosaurus, which lived in the same area. Tarbosaurus was three times the size of Therizinosaurus.

STRENGTH: 7
This dinosaur had a strong, muscular body and would have been a very powerful animal indeed.

ARMOR: 0
Therizinosaurus had no body armor, but its bladelike claws would have put off many predators.

SPEED: 6
A relative of the ostrich dinosaurs, Therizinosaurus moved upright on its two back legs and is likely to have been a fast runner.

AGILITY: 7
Therizinosaurus was probably an adaptable animal, able to reach up into the trees for food as well as forage on the ground.

SCARINESS: 7
Therizinosaurus was large and may have weighed as much as 3 tons. A dinosaur this size wielding massive claws was a formidable enemy.

SPECIAL SKILLS: 5
Some experts think the dinosaur may have used its claws to tear down termite mounds so it could feast on the insects inside.

DASPLETOSAURUS
aka TOUGH GUY

Daspletosaurus was a tiddler compared with its relative Tyrannosaurus, but still a savage hunter. With larger teeth than any other tyrannosaur, a muscular body, and a talent for ambushing its foes, Daspletosaurus could have brought down even tough monsters such as horned dinosaurs.

VITAL STATISTICS
Order: Saurischia
Family: Tyrannosauridae
Period: Late Cretaceous
Home territory: Canada
Habitat: Forest and marshland
Size: 30 ft (9 m) long

DISTINGUISHING FEATURES
Like most tyrannosaurs, Daspletosaurus had a massive head, powerful body, and sturdy back legs. It had the largest teeth of any tyrannosaur.

COMBAT HISTORY
This dinosaur was so powerful, it could attack plant-eating prey much larger than itself. It even tackled mighty horned dinosaurs such as Chasmosaurus, despite its armor of bony neck frills and spikes.

STRENGTH: 9
This brawny animal had immensely strong jaws and legs and a muscular body. Only its puny little arms let it down.

ARMOR: 0
Tyrannosaurs like Daspletosaurus had no need of body armor. Other animals ran away without even stopping to think about attacking this menacing creature.

SPEED: 7
Daspletosaurus walked upright on its two back legs and could run at speeds of 20 mph (30 km/h) or more when chasing prey.

AGILITY: 8
This dinosaur weighed as much as 7–10 tons, but despite its bulk was quick on its feet and expert at avoiding the horns and claws of struggling prey.

SCARINESS: 9
The name Daspletosaurus means "frightful lizard." All the animals in the area, except other tyrannosaurs, would have fled in terror at the approach of this blood-thirsty predator.

SPECIAL SKILLS: 9
Daspletosaurus may have often ambushed its prey. Having spied a group of plant-eating dinosaurs, the hunter would lurk silently until something came close before making its lethal pounce.

BATTLE TACTIC: AGILITY

Dinosaurs, just like animals today, needed to have every tactic at their disposal so they could catch prey or escape from danger. Many smaller meat-eaters depended on their agility, both to outmaneuver larger hunters and to get the better of prey. Creatures such as dromaeosaurs were sprightly enough to leap onto huge plant-eaters and deliver vicious bites while avoiding lashing tails. Even tyrannosaurs, with their huge bulk, were able to duck and dive to escape the struggles of their victims. Peaceful plant-eaters had to be just as agile as the predators that pursued them in order to escape their clutches.

Elasmosaurus, a fast-moving marine hunter, was an expert swimmer and very agile in the water. When hunting speedy fish darting in all directions, it was vital for a marine reptile to be able to turn quickly and seize prey with a lightning lunge of its long neck.

The fastest dinosaurs moved upright on long back legs. The leg bones were slender and light, and powered by big, strong muscles in the thigh that pulled the leg back, driving the body forward. The bones of the ankle were also long and, together with the bones of the foot, acted as the final part of the lever that pushed a high-speed runner along. Dinosaurs such as Stenonychosaurus also had a long tail that helped balance the weight of the front of the body, allowing them to run on two legs.

Like many armored dinosaurs, Talarurus had a lethal weapon in the form of a bony club at the end of its tail. The dinosaur could lash this against an attacker and easily break a few bones. In order to swing its heavy club—which could weigh as much as 55 lbs (25 kg)—Talarurus needed heavy hipbones and powerful muscles.

PACHYCEPHALOSAURUS
aka HELMET

DANGER LEVEL
5.7

Pachycephalosaurus belonged to the group of dinosaurs known as boneheads. These animals lived in herds and were peaceful plant-eaters, but rival males fought fierce head-butting battles in the mating season.

BONUS FEATURE:
THE DOME
The dome-shaped lump of solid bone on this dinosaur's head acted like a built-in crash helmet to protect its skull in battles.

VITAL STATISTICS
Order: Ornithischia
Family: Pachycephalosauridae
Period: Late Cretaceous
Home territory: North America
Habitat: Forests
Size: 15 ft (4 m)

DISTINGUISHING FEATURES
The biggest of the bonehead dinosaurs, Pachycephalosaurus had a beefy body and long, heavy tail. Its back legs were sturdy and strong, but its front legs were extremely short.

COMBAT HISTORY
This bonehead had a good sense of smell and sharp eyesight, which helped it avoid menacing meat-eaters like Albertosaurus. It had no sharp claws or horns to defend itself, so escape was its best defense. If all else failed, it could try to injure an attacker by crashing into it with its bony skull.

STRENGTH: 8
The backbone of this dinosaur was particularly strong, with special joints that kept the vertebrae from twisting out of shape during head-crashing battles. Pachycephalosaurus also had extra ribs lining its belly to help strengthen this part of the body.

ARMOR: 8
Pachycephalosaurus's skullcap was an amazing 10 inches (25 cm) thick. The dinosaur could use this bony dome to ram attackers.

SPEED: 3
Pachycephalosaurus walked upright on its back legs, but was not a very fast runner.

AGILITY: 3
Pachycephalosaurus held its heavy tail straight out behind it to balance the weight of its domed head.

SCARINESS: 6
This dinosaur was not usually fierce, but when it lowered its domed head, it looked like an animal to avoid.

SPECIAL SKILLS: 6
When charging an enemy, whether a rival male or a predator, Pachycephalosaurus held its head down and its tail straight out, then ran as fast as it could to ram its bony skull into its opponent. It may have rammed the enemy's side rather than its head—which was less likely to cause damage to itself.

TOROSAURUS

aka **SKULL**

This huge horned dinosaur lived in herds and spent most of its time quietly munching plants. With its massive horns and neck frill it was a daunting prospect for any predator.

BONUS FEATURE:
THE FRILL

The gigantic frill extending from the back of this dinosaur's neck measured more than 8 feet (2.5 meters) long.

VITAL STATISTICS

Order: Ornithischia
Family: Ceratopsidae
Period: Late Cretaceous
Home territory: North America
Habitat: Forests
Size: 25 ft (8 m) long

DISTINGUISHING FEATURES

Torosaurus was one of the largest horned dinosaurs. For many years, its skull was said to be the biggest of any known land animal, but a Pentaceratops skull has now been found that is even bigger.

COMBAT HISTORY

Even Tyrannosaurus would think twice about attacking big and burly Torosaurus. The predator's only chance was to take advantage of an animal that was already wounded and weak after a battle with a rival male.

STRENGTH: 9

Like all horned dinosaurs, Torosaurus was an enormously strong animal—it had to be to carry its own body armor around!

ARMOR: 8

As well as the neck frill, Torosaurus had two long, sharp horns above its eyes and a shorter horn on its nose, which helped it defend itself.

SPEED: 3

Torosaurus was not the speediest dinosaur. It had the legs of a plodder, not a fast runner.

AGILITY: 5

Despite its bulk, Torosaurus was quick to defend itself and use its horns against attackers.

SCARINESS: 7

Already an awesome sight, Torosaurus had another trick up its sleeve. The two holes in its crest were filled with skin that flushed bloodred when the animal was angry.

★ SPECIAL SKILLS: 6

If threatened, Torosaurus would stamp the ground with a mighty hoof and lower its huge horned head to warn off its attacker. This would have sent all but the most confident predators running for cover.

PANOPLOSAURUS

aka SHIELD

DANGER LEVEL 6.5

Panoplosaurus belonged to a family of armored dinosaurs called nodosaurs. These tanklike creatures were nowhere near as fierce as they looked and fed only on plants.

BONUS FEATURE:
CHAIN MAIL
An impressive array of studs, spikes, and bony plates made Panoplosaurus a challenge for any predator.

VITAL STATISTICS
Order: Ornithischia
Family: Nodosauridae
Period: Late Cretaceous
Home territory: North America
Habitat: Woodland
Size: 23 ft (7 m)

DISTINGUISHING FEATURES
Like all nodosaurs, Panoplosaurus was covered with flat plates of bone set into its thick skin. It also had bony plates on its head and massive spikes guarding its shoulders and sides. This dinosaur had a bulky body, thick legs, and a narrow head.

COMBAT HISTORY
If possible, Tyrannosaurus and other predators that lived alongside Panoplosaurus would go for easier prey rather than attack this tank. Their only hope was to go for the dinosaur's unprotected belly, but they ran the risk of getting stabbed by its spikes.

STRENGTH: 9
Panoplosaurus was extremely strong and could stand its ground against most attackers. It probably weighed as much as 3.5 tons.

ARMOR: 10
This dinosaur was so well armored it's a wonder any predator dared go near it. It was very difficult to get past these defenses.

SPEED: 2
Toughness rather than speed was Panoplosaurus's strategy. This dinosaur walked on four legs and was not a fast runner.

AGILITY: 4
Although not speedy, Panoplosaurus was agile enough to turn quickly to use its armor to best advantage.

SCARINESS: 7
It was a brave creature that wasn't afraid of this spiked, armor-plated monster. It might not have had sharp teeth and claws, but Panoplosaurus certainly didn't look friendly!

SPECIAL SKILLS: 7
If attacked, Panoplosaurus could twist and turn its body and drive its shoulder spikes into its enemy, causing severe wounds.

TSINTAOSAURUS
aka THE ALIEN

Tsintaosaurus was a duckbill. Duckbills were a group of plant-eating dinosaurs that were very common in the Late Cretaceous. All of these animals had crests or bumps on their heads.

BONUS FEATURE:
FLAGPOLE

Some experts think there was a flap of skin like a flag on its horn, perhaps used for signaling to other members of the herd.

VITAL STATISTICS

Order: Ornithischia
Family: Hadrosauridae
Period: Late Cretaceous
Home territory: Asia
Habitat: Forests
Size: 33 ft (10 m) long

DISTINGUISHING FEATURES

Like all duckbills, Tsintaosaurus was a large, heavily built dinosaur with a burly body and deep tail. The front of its jaws formed a long, flat beak, similar to the beak of a duck.

COMBAT HISTORY

Duckbills were preyed on by gangs of small meat-eaters such as Velociraptor, as well as bigger predators. Although Tsintaosaurus towered over the Velociraptors, they would soon have swarmed all over its body, tearing its flesh until the big creature was mortally wounded.

STRENGTH: 6
This massive creature did not have any particular weapons but was strong enough to put up a fight if attacked.

ARMOR: 0
Tsintaosaurus had no body armor with which to defend itself.

SPEED: 8
Although this dinosaur often moved around on all fours while it was feeding, it could rear up on its back legs to flee from danger. Its heavy tail helped balance its body when it stood upright.

AGILITY: 6
Tsintaosaurus had a long, flexible neck that helped it gather plants from a wide area.

SCARINESS: 4
Despite their size, duckbills like Tsintaosaurus weren't really scary, but they could make a loud booming call.

SPECIAL SKILLS: 6
Tsintaosaurus lived in herds and relied on strength in numbers. If one animal sensed danger, it would soon sound the alarm for the others.

SPECIAL SKILL: HERD INSTINCT

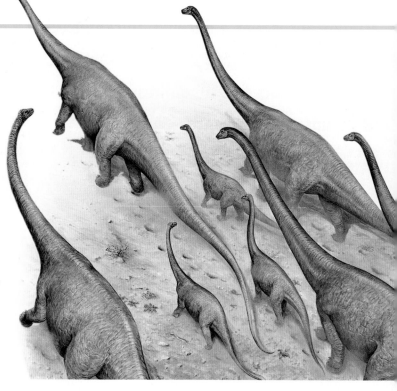

Many plant-eating animals today live in herds. Creatures such as zebra, deer, and antelope find that life is safer in a group, where there's always someone keeping an eye out for danger.

It was just the same for plant-eating dinosaurs such as duckbills, sauropods, and horned dinosaurs. Together, the dinosaurs were safer from predators and they could warn one another of approaching hunters. Dinosaur experts know that many kinds of dinosaurs lived in herds from the fossilized footprints that have been found. In some places, large numbers of prints show that adult and young dinosaurs moved together.

Some meat-eaters also found that living in groups was an advantage. Together, small predators such as dromaeosaurs could attack prey much larger than themselves.

As a herd of dinosaurs traveled together in search of food, adults walked on the outside of the group and younger animals stayed in the center, where they were protected. Predators usually picked their victims from the edges of a herd.

If a dangerous predator approached them, horned dinosaurs such as Triceratops would take extra care to defend their young. The older members would make a protective circle around the young and shake their huge horned heads at the hunter. At the sight of this, even a tyrannosaur would usually change its mind!

Like most plant-eaters today, duckbill dinosaurs had keen senses of sight, smell, and hearing. If a Parasaurolophus spotted a predator, it could make a loud honking noise, maybe amplified by the hollow crest on its head, to warn others in the herd and give them time to escape.

STYRACOSAURUS
aka CHARGER

DANGER LEVEL **7.3**

This horned dinosaur had a massive head shielded by a huge bony neck frill, ringed with mighty spikes. Like all horned dinosaurs, Styracosaurus was a herd-living plant-eater.

BONUS FEATURE:
THE HORN
This dinosaur saw off attackers with the straight horn which grew on its nose and measured up to 2 feet (60 cm) long.

VITAL STATISTICS
Order: Ornithischia
Family: Ceratopsidae
Period: Late Cretaceous
Home territory: North America
Habitat: Woodland
Size: 18 ft (5 m) long

DISTINGUISHING FEATURES
Styracosaurus's neck frill was adorned with six mighty spikes around the edges. Its body was bulky and its tail short and thick.

COMBAT HISTORY
Tyrannosaurs such as Albertosaurus would certainly have thought twice about attacking this spiky monster. But if a predator could manage to avoid Styracosaurus's weapons and get at its unprotected belly and hindquarters, it could inflict lethal wounds.

STRENGTH: 8
This dinosaur probably weighed 2 or 3 tons and needed immensely strong muscles to shake its huge head at enemies.

ARMOR: 9
Its spiky neck frill and long nose horn were good protection from predators, who would have had to be very agile if they wanted to get close to this dinosaur without injury.

SPEED: 6
Styracosaurus may have been able to run fairly fast on its short, stumpy legs, reaching speeds of up to 20 mph (32 km/h).

AGILITY: 5
Styracosaurus was nimble enough to swing around and turn on an attacker with surprising speed.

SCARINESS: 8
With its neck frill and array of spikes and horns, Styracosaurus was such an awesome creature that many animals would have fled at the mere sight of it. This meant the dinosaur probably did not have to fight too many battles.

SPECIAL SKILLS: 8
If in danger, Styracosaurus would lower its mighty horned head and charge toward its enemy like a giant rhinoceros. An animal with any sense would get out of the way as fast as it could.

SHANTUNGOSAURUS

aka BILL

This massive creature was one of the biggest of all the duckbill dinosaurs. Duckbills were common dinosaurs in Late Cretaceous Asia and huge herds of these creatures roamed the woodlands feasting on plants.

BONUS FEATURE:
THE BEAK

Like all duckbills, this dinosaur had a long, flattened beak at the front of its jaws, which it used for cropping plants.

VITAL STATISTICS

Order: Ornithischia
Family: Hadrosauridae
Period: Late Cretaceous
Home territory: Asia
Habitat: Woodland and swamps
Size: 43 ft (13 m) long

DISTINGUISHING FEATURES

Shantungosaurus had a big, deep body and an enormously long tail, which measured up to half its total body length. Its head was long and flat, and it had no horn or crest.

COMBAT HISTORY

Duckbills were the main prey of tyrannosaurs and even an animal the size of Shantungosaurus could be overcome by a tyrannosaur's daggerlike teeth. Gangs of smaller predators such as Velociraptor might also have attacked Shantungosaurus.

STRENGTH: 7

This was a powerfully built animal, weighing as much as 4.5 tons, with a strong neck.

ARMOR: 0

Shantungosaurus had no body armor and depended on its great bulk for protection.

SPEED: 6

This dinosaur probably spent most of its time on all fours while it fed, but could rear up on its back legs to run away from danger when necessary.

AGILITY: 5

Shantungosaurus's heavy tail helped balance its body weight when it walked upright.

SCARINESS: 6

Although Shantungosaurus had no particular weapons, a herd of these massive creatures, each one three times the height of today's elephant, would have been an impressive sight.

SPECIAL SKILLS: 6

Herding dinosaurs like Shantungosaurus relied on safety in numbers. When one dinosaur sounded the alarm that a predator was in the area, all the animals in the herd would rear up on two legs and flee from danger as fast as possible. Shantungosaurus, like all plant-eaters, preferred to stay well away from trouble.

TRICERATOPS

aka HORNS

One of the largest and most common horned dinosaurs, Triceratops was at least twice the length of today's rhinoceros and weighed up to 10 tons. Its huge skull alone was more than 6 feet (1.8 meters) long.

BONUS FEATURE:
THREE HORNS
Two big, sharp horns on the top of its head and one on its nose helped Triceratops protect itself from enemies.

VITAL STATISTICS
Order: Ornithischia
Family: Ceratopsidae
Period: Late Cretaceous
Home territory: North America
Habitat: Woodland
Size: 30 ft (9 m) long

DISTINGUISHING FEATURES
This colossal creature had a bulky body, heavy, pillarlike legs, and a short, bony neck frill. Like all horned dinosaurs, it had a strong beak at the front of its jaws.

COMBAT HISTORY
Tyrannosaurs were Triceratops's main enemies, but even they were wary and stalked this monster very carefully. Their best chance was to attack a Triceratops that was already wounded after a battle with a rival male in the breeding season.

STRENGTH: 10
Enormously strong animals, rival males would engage in titanic struggles, locking horns and pushing one another with their bony neck shields.

ARMOR: 10
Triceratops was extremely well protected. Its brow horns were more than 3 feet (1 meter) long, and the short horn on its nose measured about 7 inches (20 cm). Its neck frill was a solid sheet of bone that acted as a shield for its vulnerable neck and shoulders.

SPEED: 2
This dinosaur was not a fast runner, but did not need to rely on speed for defense.

AGILITY: 5
Triceratops was too heavy to rear up on two legs, but was able to maneuver its hulking head against an attacker.

SCARINESS: 8
A terrifying creature. Although Triceratops fed only on plants and did not look for trouble, it did not hesitate to use its battery of weapons if attacked.

SPECIAL SKILLS: 8
Triceratops would stand its ground against a predator. If the hunter came too near, Triceratops would lower its head and charge, holding its huge horns at the ready to pierce the enemy's flesh.

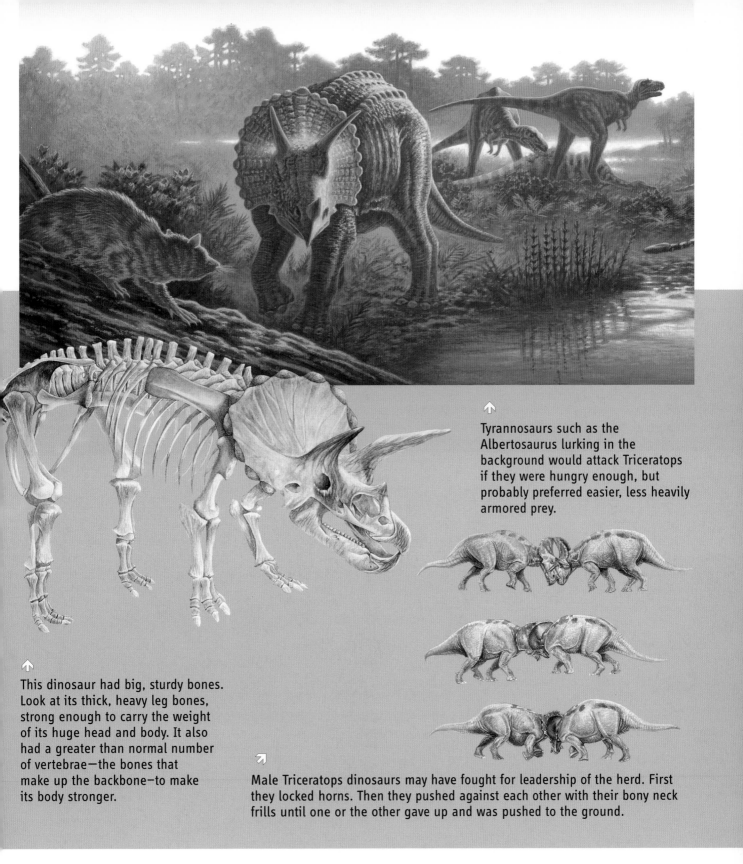

Tyrannosaurs such as the Albertosaurus lurking in the background would attack Triceratops if they were hungry enough, but probably preferred easier, less heavily armored prey.

This dinosaur had big, sturdy bones. Look at its thick, heavy leg bones, strong enough to carry the weight of its huge head and body. It also had a greater than normal number of vertebrae—the bones that make up the backbone—to make its body stronger.

Male Triceratops dinosaurs may have fought for leadership of the herd. First they locked horns. Then they pushed against each other with their bony neck frills until one or the other gave up and was pushed to the ground.

TYRANNOSAURUS

aka **REX**

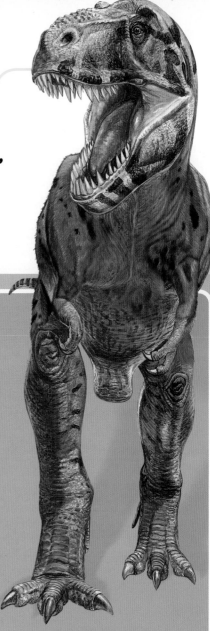

One of the most ferocious killers the world has ever known, Tyrannosaurus was king of the Cretaceous. Its name means "tyrant lizard" and was richly deserved. This bloodthirsty monster terrorized virtually all other animals of the time.

VITAL STATISTICS
Order: Saurischia
Family: Tyrannosauridae
Period: Late Cretaceous
Home territory: North America
Habitat: Most lowland areas
Size: Up to 43 ft (13 m) long

DISTINGUISHING FEATURES
Tyrannosaurus stood up to 20 feet (7 meters) tall. It had strong jaws lined with jagged teeth up to 9 inches (25 cm) long. Scientists think it may have had a covering of feathers.

COMBAT HISTORY
Huge duckbills such as Edmontosaurus were common prey, and this monster could even get the better of Styracosaurus and other armored prey. But like lions today, Tyrannosaurus was also a scavenger and would feast on creatures that were already dead.

STRENGTH: 10
Tyrannosaurus weighed up to 5 tons and was immensely strong. With one bite it could crush an animal's bones. And it could gulp down 150 lbs (70 kg) of meat in one go!

ARMOR: 8
Tyrannosaurus had no body armor, but what animal was foolish enough to attack a creature with a mouthful of teeth like steak knives?

SPEED: 5
The one weakness of this giant killer was its lack of speed. Its bulk made it hard for it to run at more than about 20 mph (30 km/h), so it was difficult for Tyrannosaurus to chase fast-moving prey.

AGILITY: 8
Despite its lack of speed, Tyrannosaurus was reasonably agile, able to leap and turn quickly when battling with prey.

SCARINESS: 10
Tyrannosaurus was the scariest of all dinosaurs—a menacing monster that struck fear into all it met.

SPECIAL SKILLS: 10
With its huge, heavy body, Tyrannosaurus could not chase prey for long. Instead it stayed hidden among the trees, watching for a likely victim. If unsuspecting prey came near, Tyrannosaurus would leap out, charge toward its prey, and pounce, delivering lethal bites to the animal's neck.

Tyrannosaurus's jaws alone were more than 3 feet (1 meter) long and equipped with as many as 60 razor-sharp teeth. Like steak knives, they were ideal for slicing into flesh.

Tyrannosaurus surprises a herd of Corythosaurus. As the monster thunders into view, the peaceful plant-eaters look up in alarm and get ready to run—fast!

THE CHAMPS

Tyrannosaurs were the largest land carnivores that have ever lived. As well as Tyrannosaurus, there were other monsters such as Alioramus, Siamotyrannus, Albertosaurus, and Tarbosaurus, all of which were nearly as big and just as ferocious.

Unlike smaller killers such as Velociraptor and Dromaeosaurus, tyrannosaurs did not have long vicious claws for killing their prey. They depended on their incredibly powerful jaws and teeth. The jaws were so strong and the teeth so sharp that a tyrannosaur could carve out a huge chunk of its victim's flesh in seconds and swallow it whole. Even tyrannosaurs had their problems, though. One fossil of a large carnivore has been found that shows the animal had two large bones stuck in its throat. The tyrannosaur was so greedy it choked to death!

THE BATTLE

TIME:
Late Cretaceous

PLACE:
North America

WINNER:
Tyrannosaurus

TYRANNOSAURUS vs. TRICERATOPS

With its huge horns and neck shield, Triceratops is a daunting enemy—even for Tyrannosaurus. But this monster is hungry and Triceratops is the only prey around. Tyrannosaurus tries its ambush technique and manages to sink its teeth into the horned dinosaur's side, tearing off a lump of flesh. But Triceratops wheels swiftly around and turns its horns on Tyrannosaurus. The predator retreats for a while and waits. Triceratops is bleeding heavily and growing weaker. Despite its pain, Triceratops tries one last charge on its enemy. But Tyrannosaurus is ready and delivers yet more crushing bites. Triceratops is too weak to fight back and soon the battle is over.

THE BATTLE
TIME:
65 million years ago
PLACE:
The world
WINNER:
Extinction

DINOSAURS vs. EXTINCTION

No one knows exactly what happened 65 million years ago, when dinosaurs and many other creatures disappeared forever. Some experts think that dinosaurs and other creatures had started dying out several million years before the final extinction. This may have been because the climate had become cooler, partly because lots of volcanic eruptions threw great quantities of dust into the atmosphere, and the lives of animals were affected.

Other experts are convinced that the extinctions were caused by a huge meteorite that struck Earth around 65 million years ago. The debris caused by such an impact would have darkened the skies for many years. Many plants, both on land and in the sea, would have died from lack of light. Plant-eating dinosaurs could not survive without enough food so also died, followed by the carnivores that fed on them.

It's possible that both theories are right and that the dinosaurs were already dying out before the meteor brought their final dramatic end.

A meteorite is a lump of rock from outer space that enters the Earth's atmosphere and lands on Earth. A huge meteorite, measuring at least 6 miles (10 kilometers) across, struck the Earth at the end of the Cretaceous. A crater from this time, that could have been made by such an impact, has been discovered in Mexico. Also, rocks of that time from all over the world contain unusual minerals that could only have come from a meteorite, from the debris thrown up after the enormous impact.

The world was rocked with a high number of volcanic eruptions toward the end of the Cretaceous. Huge amounts of dust and debris were thrown into the air, darkening the sky and blocking out sunlight. As more and more plants died, so did plant-eating dinosaurs. Meat-eaters could survive for a while, feeding on the dead bodies, but soon there was no prey and they too starved to death.

WHAT DIED AND WHAT SURVIVED

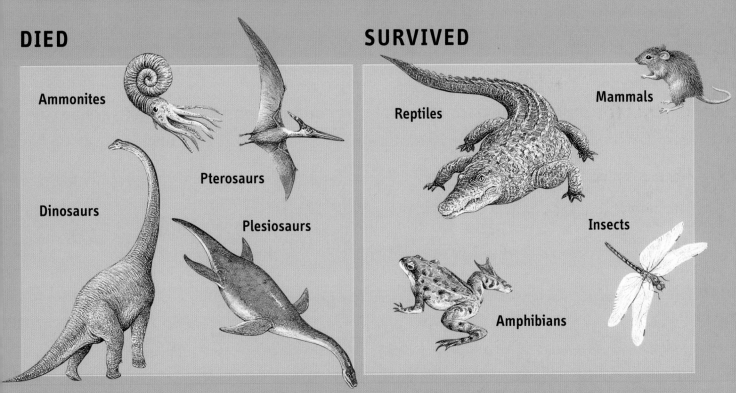

DIED

Ammonites

Pterosaurs

Dinosaurs

Plesiosaurs

SURVIVED

Reptiles

Mammals

Insects

Amphibians

As well as dinosaurs, animals such as ammonites, pterosaurs, and many marine reptiles disappeared forever. Creatures that managed to survive the mass extinction included other kinds of reptiles, such as crocodiles, lizards, and snakes, as well as mammals, amphibians, and insects.

SCORE TABLE

Below are the top scorers for each of the battle tactics. Opposite are the top overall scorers. Not all of these are blood-thirsty hunters. Some are high scorers because of their great strength or incredible armor and weapons. No one knows exactly what went on in the days of the dinosaurs, but it's fun to imagine some of the ferocious battles that may have taken place.

BATTLE TACTICS

⚔ STRENGTH

NAME	PERIOD	TERRITORY	PAGE	SCORE
Apatosaurus	Late Jurassic	North America	70	10
Diplodocus	Late Jurassic	North America	68–69	10
Seismosaurus	Late Jurassic	North America	74	10
Tyrannosaurus	Late Cretaceous	North America	130–131	10
Triceratops	Late Cretaceous	North America	128–129	10

🛡 ARMOR

NAME	PERIOD	TERRITORY	PAGE	SCORE
Panoplosaurus	Late Cretaceous	North America	122	10
Triceratops	Late Cretaceous	North America	128–129	10
Euoplocephalus	Late Cretaceous	North America	96	9
Sauropelta	Early Cretaceous	North America	89	9
Styracosaurus	Late Cretaceous	North America	126	9

⏱ SPEED

NAME	PERIOD	TERRITORY	PAGE	SCORE
Dromaeosaurus	Late Cretaceous	North America	97	9
Dromiceiomimus	Late Cretaceous	North America	122	9
Velociraptor	Late Cretaceous	Asia	110	9
Mosasaurus hoffmani	Late Cretaceous	Europe, North America, Africa, Australia, New Zealand	114–115	9
Quetzalcoatlus	Late Cretaceous	North America	106	8

⚡ AGILITY

NAME	PERIOD	TERRITORY	PAGE	SCORE
Dromiceiomimus	Late Cretaceous	North America	112	9
Kronosaurus	Early Cretaceous	Australia	85	9
Dromaeosaurus	Late Cretaceous	North America	97	9
Velociraptor	Late Cretaceous	Asia	110	9
Mosasaurus hoffmani	Late Cretaceous	Europe, North America, Africa, Australia, New Zealand	114–115	8

☠ SCARINESS

NAME	PERIOD	TERRITORY	PAGE	SCORE
Diplodocus	Late Jurassic	North America	68–69	10
Apatosaurus	Late Jurassic	North America	70	10
Seismosaurus	Late Jurassic	North America	74	10
Tyrannosaurus	Late Cretaceous	North America	130–131	10
Megalosaurus	Jurassic	Europe, Africa	78–79	10

★ SPECIAL SKILLS

NAME	PERIOD	TERRITORY	PAGE	SCORE
Apatosaurus	Late Jurassic	North America	70	10
Giganotosaurus	Late Cretaceous	South America	107	10
Tyrannosaurus	Late Cretaceous	North America	130–131	10
Deinosuchus	Late Cretaceous	North America	101	9
Mamenchisaurus	Late Jurassic	Asia: Mongolia	62	9

TOP TEN DANGER LEVEL SCORERS

NAME	PERIOD	TERRITORY	DEFEATED	PAGE	SCORE
Tyrannosaurus	Late Cretaceous	North America	Triceratops	130–131	8.5
Giganotosaurus	Late Cretaceous	South America	Saltasaurus	107	8.3
Deinosuchus	Late Cretaceous	North America	Tarbosaurus	101	8.3
Suchomimus	Early Cretaceous	Africa	Algoasaurus	111	7.8
Kronosaurus	Early Cretaceous	Australia	Platypterygius	85	7.5
Megalosaurus	Jurassic	Europe, Africa	Cetiosaurus	78–79	7.3
Styracosaurus	Late Cretaceous	North America	Albertosaurus	126	7.3
Triceratops	Late Cretaceous	North America	Albertosaurus	128–129	7.2
Mosasaurus hoffmani	Late Cretaceous	Europe, North America, Africa, Australia, New Zealand	Elasmosaurus	114–115	7.1
Daspletosaurus	Late Cretaceous	Canada	Chasmosaurus	117	7

PERIOD PLAY-OFFS

Each period in the days of the dinosaurs produced creatures that were bigger and fiercer than ever before. If we imagine that the top dinosaurs from different periods could have fought each other, the ultimate champ would have been Tyrannosaurus from the Cretaceous period, the most ferocious predator the world has ever known.

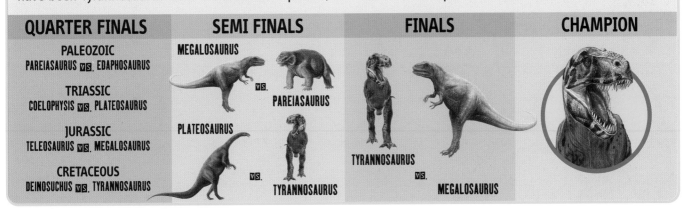

QUARTER FINALS	SEMI FINALS	FINALS	CHAMPION
PALEOZOIC PAREIASAURUS VS. EDAPHOSAURUS	MEGALOSAURUS VS. PAREIASAURUS	TYRANNOSAURUS VS. MEGALOSAURUS	
TRIASSIC COELOPHYSIS VS. PLATEOSAURUS			
JURASSIC TELEOSAURUS VS. MEGALOSAURUS	PLATEOSAURUS VS. TYRANNOSAURUS		
CRETACEOUS DEINOSUCHUS VS. TYRANNOSAURUS			

GLOSSARY

Ammonite An extinct relative of today's octopus and squid. An ammonite was a soft-bodied animal with tentacles that lived inside a hard-coiled shell.

Amphibian A four-legged animal with a backbone that lays its eggs in water. A young amphibian passes through a stage as a swimming tadpole before becoming an adult that can live on land. Frogs, toads, and newts are examples of amphibians today.

Ankylosaur A member of a group of armored dinosaurs, with a heavy ball of bone like a club at the end of its tail.

Armored dinosaur Armored dinosaurs were covered with plates of bone and bony spikes which helped protect them from predators. There were two kinds of armored dinosaurs—ankylosaurs and nodosaurs. Euoplocephalus and Sauropelta were both armored dinosaurs.

Boneheaded dinosaur A boneheaded dinosaur had an unusual dome-shaped skull. Inside was a solid lump of bone that acted like a crash helmet to protect the dinosaur's head in battles.

Pachycephalosaurus was a boneheaded dinosaur.

Carnivore An animal that feeds on the flesh of other animals.

Cretaceous The period from 146 to 65 million years ago.

Cycad A cone-bearing plant that lived before flowering plants. A cycad had a short thick trunk and long palmlike leaves.

Duckbill dinosaur A duckbill was a plant-eating dinosaur with a long, flattened beak at the front of its jaws. The dinosaur used this beak for uprooting and gathering plants. Tsintaosaurus and Parasaurolophus were both duckbill dinosaurs.

Extinction The dying out of a species of plant or animal.

Family A group of a related species. For example, all the iguanodonts, such as Iguanodon and Muttaburrasaurus, belong to the family Iguanodontidae. The name of a family usually ends in "-idae."

Fossil The remains of an animal that have been preserved in rock. Hard body parts, such as bones and teeth, are more likely to form fossils than soft parts such as organs. Impressions in rocks, such as footprints, can also become fossilized.

Horned dinosaur A horned dinosaur had a large head with long, pointed horns. Most also had a huge sheet of bone called a frill at the back of their head that helped protect the dinosaur from predators. Triceratops and Chasmosaurus were both horned dinosaurs.

Jurassic The period from 200 to 146 million years ago.

Mammal A four-legged animal with a backbone that has hair on its body and feeds its young on milk produced in its own body. Animals such as cats, horses, monkeys, and humans are all mammals.

Nodosaur A member of a group of armored dinosaurs, with long spikes sticking out to the sides of its body.

Order An order is a group of related families. There are two orders of dinosaurs—Ornithischia and Saurischia. The dinosaurs in the two orders differ in the structure of their hipbones.

Ornithischia One of the two orders of dinosaurs. All ornithischian dinosaurs were plant-eaters.

Paleozoic The era from 550 to 250 million years ago.

Predator An animal that hunts and kills animals for food.

Prey An animal hunted by a predator.

Pterosaur A flying reptile that lived at the same time as the dinosaurs. Pterosaurs had wings made of skin attached to extra-long fingers on each hand. Examples of pterosaurs include Quetzalcoatlus and Rhamphorhynchus.

Reptile A four-legged animal with a backbone that has a dry skin and breathes air. Most reptiles lay eggs with tough leathery shells. These eggs hatch into young that look like small versions of their parents. Snakes, lizards, and crocodiles are all examples of reptiles today.

Saurischia One of the two orders of dinosaurs. Saurischians included meat-eating and plant-eating dinosaurs.

Sauropod A huge, long-necked, plant-eating dinosaur. Sauropods were the largest known dinosaurs and included animals such as Diplodocus and Brachiosaurus.

Species A type of plant or animal. Members of the same species can mate and produce young that can themselves have young.

Triassic The period from 250 to 200 million years ago.

Vertebra One of the bones that make up an animal's backbone.

INDEX

NOTE: Page numbers in *italic* refer to illustrations. Main references are in **bold**.

A

Acrocanthosaurus 89
aetosaurs 31
Alamosaurus *77*
Albertosaurus *82*, 112, 113, 120, 126, *129*, 131
Alioramus 104, 116, 131
Allosaurus 13, 49, **56–57**, 60, 68, 70, 74, 77, 108
Amargasaurus 88
ammonites 49, 52, 135
amphibians 10, 135
anapsid reptiles 10, 11
Angustinaripterus 48
Anhanguera 39
ankylosaurs 13, 96, 98
Apatosaurus 70
Archaeopteryx 49
Archelon *11*, **100**
archosaurs 28, 31
Ardeosaurus *11*
armored dinosaurs 13, 96, 98, 99, 119, 122

B

Baryonx 75
battle scenes 20–21, 30–31, 42–43, 56–57, 72–73, 90–91, 102–103, 132–133
belemnites 49, *52*
birds
    earliest 49
    early oystercatcher *82*
    dinosaur relatives 91
body temperature 19, 60, 98
bonehead dinosaurs 13, 120

Brachiosaurus 13, **72–73**
Brontosaurus *see* Apatosaurus

C

Cambrian 9
Camptosaurus 71
Carboniferous period 9, 10, 11, 16
Carcharodontosaurus 77
carnivores *see* meat-eaters
carnosaurs 13, 77, 107
Carnotaurus 94
Centrosaurus *82*, *99*
ceratosaurs 26, 27
Ceratosaurus 54, **72–73**
Cetiosaurus *76*
Chasmosaurus **105**, 117
climate
    Carboniferous 16
    Cretaceous 83
    Jurassic 48
    Permian 16
    Triassic 27
Coelophysis **34–35**, 44
coelurosaurs 13
Compsognathus *76*
Corythosaurus *82*, 83, *131*
Cretaceous period 9, 12
crocodiles 11, 26, 28, 50, 106, 135
Cryolophosaurus 55
Cynognathus 30–31

D

Daspletosaurus **117**
Deinonychus 86, **90–91**, *108*
Deinosuchus **101**, 106
Desmatosuchus 31, **36**

Devonian period 9
diapsid reptiles 10, 18
Dicynodon *11*, *17*
diet
    dinosaurs 8
    plant-eaters 26, 49
Dilophosaurus 51
dinosaurs
    body temperature 19, 60, 98
    earliest 27
    extinction 83, 134
    family life 8
    feathers 8, 110, 116, 130
    herds 62, 68, 73, 124–125
    teeth 8, 21, 31, 37
    ways of moving 12
Diplodocus 13, **68–69**
dromaeosaurs 13, 118, 124
Dromaeosaurus *64*, **97**, 108, 131
Dromiceiomimus 112
duckbilled dinosaurs 13, 83, 94, 97, 111, 113, 123, 124, 125, 127, 130

E

Edaphosaurus 19
Edmontosaurus 130
egg
    amphibian 10
    plesiosaur 52
    reptile 10
Elasmosaurus *118*
Endoceras *53*
Eoraptor 42–43
Erythrosuchus 30–31
Eudimorphodon *26*, **37**
Euoplocephalus 96

Euparkeria 28
Eurinosaurus *52*
extinction 83, 134

F

family life 8
feathers 8, 110, 116, 130
feeding
  meat-eaters 49, 77, 108, 134, 135
    Anhanguera *39*
    Ceratosaurus *72–73*
    Coelophysis *35*
    Deinonychus *90–91*
    Dromaeosaurus *64*
    Endoceras *53*
    Erythrosuchus *30*
    Gasosaurus *48*
    Herrerasaurus *42–43*
    Ichthyosaurus *52*
    Lycaenops *20–21*
    Megalosaurus 79
    plesiosaurs *52*
    Tarbosaurus *102–103, 108–109*
    Troodon *82*
    Tyrannosaurus *131, 132–133*
  plant-eaters 48–49, 69, 134,
    135
    Iguanodon *87*
    Stegosaurus *61*
flying reptiles *see* pterosaurs
fossils 8, 79, 124, 131

G

Gallimimus *65*, **102–103**,
  109
Gasosaurus *48*, 49, 58

Giganotosaurus 107
Gondwana 16, 49

H

herds 62, 68, 73, 124–125
Herrerasaurus 42–43
horned dinosaurs 13, 83, 95, 105,
  121, 124, 125, 126, 128
Hovasaurus 23
Huayangosaurus 48
Hylonomus 10, 11, 16
Hypsognathus 44
Hysilophodon *87*, **90–91**

I

ichthyosaurs 11, 33, 49, 52, *53*, 66,
  83, 85, 100
  birth 52
Ichthyosaurus *52*
Iguanodon *12*, **86–87**
iguanodonts 13, 94
insects 135

J

Jurassic period 9

K

Kentrosaurus 56–57
Kronosaurus 85

L

Laurasia 49
Laurentia 16
Leaellynasaura 84
lepidotes *52*
Lesothosaurus 54

Lexovisaurus 59
Liliensternus *26*, 27
Liopleurodon 66
lizards 82, 135
  earliest 11
  ways of moving 12
Lufengosaurus 58
Lycaenops *16*, *17*,
  20–21
Lystrosaurus *16*

M

Mamenchisaurus 62
mammal-like reptiles 11, 16, 21
mammals 135
maps
  Carboniferous world 17
  Cretaceous world 83
  Jurassic world 49
  Triassic world 27
Marasuchus 32
marine reptiles 11, 29, 33, 40, 49, 52,
  66, 135
meat-eaters 49, 55, 77, 124, 131,
  134, 135
Megalosaurus 49, 59, **78–79**,
  87
meteorite 83, 134
Milleretta *16*
mosasaurs 114
Moschops 20–21
Mosasaurus hoffmani 114–115

N

nodosaurs 13, 98, 122
nothosaurs 40

O

Ophthalmosaurus 66
Ordovician period 9, 53
ornithischians 12, 13
Ornitholestes *12*
ornithomimids 13
Ornithomimus *65*
Ornithosuchus 31
Ouranosaurus 92
oystercatcher, early *82*

P

Pachycephalosaurus 120
pack hunters 56, 97, 110, 124
Paleozoic period 9
Pangaea 16, 26, 27,
    49
Panoplosaurus 122
Parasaurolophus **113**, *125*
Pareiasaurus 22
Peltobatrachus *16*
Pentaceratops **95**, 121
Permian period 9, 16
Peteinosaurus *26*
Petrolacosaurus 18
phytosaurs 31
Pistosaurus 40
placodonts 29
Placodus 29
plant-eaters 49, 58, 69, 77, 124,
    134, 135
Plateosaurus *26*, **41**
plesiosaurs 49, 52, 53,
    66, 114
Plesiosaurus *52*
pliosaurs 85, 100

Procynosuchus *17*
Proganochelys 45
prosauropods 26, 55
Proterosuchus 31
Protoceratops 104
Pteranodon *11*, *82*
pterodactyloids 39
Pterodaustro 63
pterosaurs (flying reptiles) 11,
    26, 27, 31, 37, *38*, *39*,
    48, 49, 63, 71, 75,
    83, 135

Q

Quetzalcoatlus 106

R

reptiles 135
    anapsid 10, 11
    aquatic 23, 31, 45
    crocodiles 11, 26, 28, 50,
        106, 135
    diapsid 10, 18
    early 9, 10, 11, 12,
        16, 22
        ways of moving 12
    early ruling 28, 31
    flying *see* pterosaurs
    mammal-like 11, 16, 21
    marine 11, 29, 33, 40, 49, 52,
        66, 135
    snakes 135
    synapsid 10
rhamphorhynchoids 39
Rhamphorynchus 71
Robertia *17*

S

Sacabambaspis *53*
Saltasaurus 77, 107
saurischians 12, 13
Saurolophus 97
Sauropelta 89
sauropods 13, 48, 49, 70,
    76, 77, 78, 107, 111, 124
Scaphognathus 75
scoring 9
Scutellosaurus 51
Seismosaurus 13, **74**
Shantungosaurus 127
Shonisaurus **33**, 40
Shunosaurus *48*
Siamotyrannus 131
Silurian 9
skeletons 10, 12, 39, 53, 61, 69,
    129
    jawbones 115
skulls 8, 9, 18
    Pachycephalosaurus 120
    Pentaceratops 121
    Tyrannosaurus 131
    Velociraptor 110
snakes 135
Spinosaurus 92
stegosaurs 13, 48, 51, 59, 60, 67,
    93, 98, *99*
Stegosaurus 60–61
Stenonychosaurus *119*
Stenopterygius *11*
Struthiomimus *65*
Styracosaurus *98*, **126**, 130
Suchomimus 111
synapsid reptiles 10

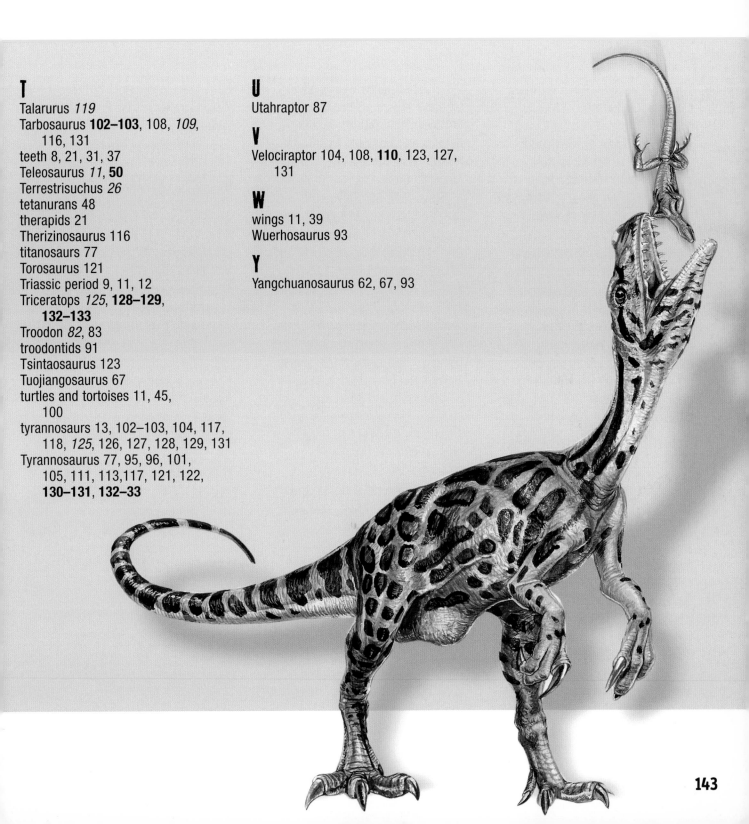

T

Talarurus *119*
Tarbosaurus **102–103**, 108, *109*,
    116, 131
teeth 8, 21, 31, 37
Teleosaurus *11*, **50**
Terrestrisuchus *26*
tetanurans 48
therapids 21
Therizinosaurus 116
titanosaurs 77
Torosaurus 121
Triassic period 9, 11, 12
Triceratops *125*, **128–129**,
    132–133
Troodon *82*, 83
troodontids 91
Tsintaosaurus 123
Tuojiangosaurus 67
turtles and tortoises 11, 45,
    100
tyrannosaurs 13, 102–103, 104, 117,
    118, *125*, 126, 127, 128, 129, 131
Tyrannosaurus 77, 95, 96, 101,
    105, 111, 113,117, 121, 122,
    130–131, **132–33**

U

Utahraptor 87

V

Velociraptor 104, 108, **110**, 123, 127,
    131

W

wings 11, 39
Wuerhosaurus 93

Y

Yangchuanosaurus 62, 67, 93

ILLUSTRATION CREDITS

t = top; b = bottom; c = center;
r = right; l = left

9tl David Bergen; 9tr Steve Kirk;
9cl Steve Kirk; 9cr Steve Kirk;
10l Steve Kirk; 10r Peter David
Scott/Wildlife Art Agency; 11 Steve
Kirk; 12l Peter David Scott/Wildlife
Art Agency; 12r Elizabeth Gray;
13 Steve Kirk; 16–17 Peter David
Scott; 17t Eugene Fleury; 18 Steve
Kirk; 19 Steve Kirk; 20 Fiammetta
Dogi; 21t Steve Kirk; 21b Steve Kirk;
22 Steve Kirk; 23 Steve Kirk;
26 James Field/Simon Girling
Associates; 27 Eugene Fleury;
28 Steve Kirk; 29 Steve Kirk;
30 Fiammetta Dogi; 31t Steve Kirk;
31b Steve Kirk; 32 Steve Kirk;
33 Steve Kirk; 34 Steve Kirk; 35
Steve Kirk; 36 Steve Kirk;
37 Steve Kirk; 38 Steve Kirk;
39t Elizabeth Gray; 39b Steve Kirk;
40 Steve Kirk; 41 Steve Kirk;
42 Fiammetta Dogi; 43t Steve Kirk;
43b Steve Kirk; 44 Steve Kirk;
45 Steve Kirk; 48 James
Field/Simon Girling Associates;
49 Eugene Fleury; 50 Steve Kirk;
51 Steve Kirk; 52 Steve Kirk; 53t Bill
Donohoe; 53b Elizabeth Gray;
54 Steve Kirk; 55 Steve Kirk;
56–57 Fiammetta Dogi; 58 Steve
Kirk; 59 Steve Kirk; 60 Steve Kirk;

61t Elizabeth Gray; 61b Steve Kirk;
62 Steve Kirk; 63 Steve Kirk;
64t Steve Kirk; 64b Steve Kirk;
65t Peter David Scott/Wildlife Art
Agency; 65cl Steve Kirk; 65cr Steve
Kirk; 65b Steve Kirk; 66 Steve Kirk;
67 Steve Kirk; 68t Steve Kirk;
68–69c Steve Kirk; 69tr Peter David
Scott/Wildlife Art Agency; Elizabeth
Gray; 70 Steve Kirk; 71 Steve Kirk;
72–73 Fiammetta Dogi; 74 Steve
Kirk; 75 Steve Kirk; 76 Steve Kirk;
77t Steve Kirk; 77b Peter David
Scott/Wildlife Art Agency; 78 Steve
Kirk; 79t Guy Smith/Mainline
Design; 79b Steve Kirk; 82 James
Field/Simon Girling Associates;
84 Steve Kirk; 85 Steve Kirk;
86 Steve Kirk; 87t Robin Boutrell/
Wildlife Art Agency; 87b Robin
Boutrell/Wildlife Art Agency;
88 Steve Kirk; 89 Steve Kirk;
90–91 Fiammetta Dogi; 92 Steve
Kirk; 93 Steve Kirk; 94 Steve Kirk;
95 Steve Kirk; 96 Steve Kirk;
97 Steve Kirk; 98 Steve Kirk;
99t Steve Kirk; 99c Steve Kirk;
99b Mark Iley; 100 Steve Kirk;
101 Steve Kirk; 102–103 Fiammetta
Dogi; 104 Steve Kirk; 105 Steve
Kirk; 106 Steve Kirk; 107 Steve
Kirk; 108 Steve Kirk; 109t Peter
David Scott; 109b Peter David
Scott/Wildlife Art Agency; 110 Steve

Kirk; 111 Steve Kirk; 112 Steve
Kirk; 113 Steve Kirk; 114–115 Peter
David Scott/Wildlife Art Agency;
116 Steve Kirk; 117 Steve Kirk;
118–119 Steve Kirk; 120 Steve Kirk;
121 Steve Kirk; 122 Steve Kirk;
123 Steve Kirk; 124 Peter David
Scott/Wildlife Art Agency; 125t Steve
Kirk; 125b Peter David Scott/Wildlife
Art Agency; 126 Steve Kirk;
127 Steve Kirk; 128 Steve Kirk;
129t Steve Kirk; 129cl Steve Kirk;
129cr Steve Kirk; 130 Steve Kirk;
131l Steve Kirk; 131tr Peter David
Scott/Wildlife Art Agency;
132–133 Fiammetta Dogi;
134 David Bergen/Virgil Pomfret
Agency; 135t David Bergen/
Virgil Pomfret Agency; 135b Peter
David Scott/Wildlife Art Agency

Feathers on dinosaurs on pages 97,
110, 112, 116, 119t, and 130 added
by Fiammetta Dogi